In-Line Skating

Mark Powell

John Svensson

Human Kinetics Publishers

Library of Congress Cataloging-in-Publication Data

Powell, Mark, 1959-
   In-line skating / by Mark Powell, John Svensson.
     p.   cm.
   Includes index.
   ISBN 0-87322-399-3
   1. In-line skating. I. Svensson, John. II. Title.
GV859.73P69 1993   92-16686
796.2'1--dc20   CIP

ISBN: 0-87322-399-3

Figure 10.1 on page 108 courtesy of the United States Confederation of Roller Skating. Photo by Steve Priest.

Cover photo courtesy of Ultra Wheels.

Human Kinetics books are available at special discounts for bulk purchase for sales promotions, premiums, fund-raising, or educational use. Special editions or book excerpts can also be created to specification. For details, contact the Special Sales Manager at Human Kinetics.

Acquisitions Editor: Brian Holding; **Developmental Editor:** Mary E. Fowler; **Assistant Editors:** Laura Bofinger and Moyra Knight; **Copyeditor:** Chris DeVito; **Proofreader:** Moyra Knight; **Indexer:** Theresa J. Schaefer; **Production Director:** Ernie Noa; **Typesetter:** Julie Overholt; **Text Design:** Keith Blomberg; **Text Layout:** Denise Lowry; **Cover Design:** Jack Davis; **Illustrations:** Cindy Butler; **Interior Photos:** Andy Barker; **Printer:** United Graphics

Printed in the United States of America   10 9 8 7 6 5

Human Kinetics
P.O. Box 5076, Champaign, IL 61825-5076
1-800-747-4457

Canada: Human Kinetics, Box 24040, Windsor, ON N8Y 4Y9
1-800-465-7301 (in Canada only)

Europe: Human Kinetics, P.O. Box IW14, Leeds LS16 6TR, England
(44) 532 781708

Australia: Human Kinetics, 2 Ingrid Street, Clapham 5062, South Australia
(08) 371 3755

New Zealand: Human Kinetics, P.O. Box 105-231, Auckland 1
(09) 309 2259

To Jonathon,
Find the things that you do well and excel at them. Keep skating, son.
 Mark Powell

To Einar Svensson,
My father, who gave me my first pair of in-line skates in 1979 and taught
me how to use them.
 John Svensson

Contents

About the Authors

Mark Powell

John Svensson

No two authors are better qualified to provide you with expert advice and information on in-line skating than Mark Powell and John Svensson.

An accomplished athlete, **Mark Powell** is a trick and dance skater who also enjoys in-line racing. He is an in-line skating instructor, an active member of the International In-Line Skate Association (IISA), and a founding member of In-Line Northwest, a Seattle-based skate club. Mark has also skied and skated competitively—winning the Inter-Mountain Skateboarding championship in 1978 and qualifying for the 10K In-Line Skating Nationals in 1991. Mark has been an active member of the Seattle Laser Fleet, a local sailing club, since November 1986.

Mark is the author of *The Complete Car Buyer's Handbook* and articles on individual participant sports. He is also an authority on direct marketing techniques for small businesses.

John Svensson is widely recognized as one of the world's top in-line skating racers. For the past two years he has been manager and captain of the Ultra Wheels race team and a research and design technician for the Ultra Wheels company. His work with Ultra Wheels has provided him with valuable knowledge on current equipment and techniques. John has tested almost every skate and skate component on the market and is considered an authority on skate design.

John also is an active member of IISA and vice president of Club In-Line Northwest. In 1991 he participated in the Coastline Roll for America's Oceans, a 1,000-mile skate along the Pacific coast. John's favorite leisure activities include in-line skating and cross-country and alpine skiing.

Preface

Welcome to *In-Line Skating*! You're about to begin a fun, health-promoting, popular new sport. The in-line skating industry has grown at a tremendous pace. In 1986 in-line skating was a $7-million industry; by 1991 it had grown to more than $200 million. As a top dance skater and recreational racer (Powell) and an experienced world class skater (Svensson), we are well suited to cover the many aspects of in-line skating, and are able to bring solid, fundamental instruction to the millions of in-line skaters around the world. Whether you're a beginner, intermediate, or advanced skater, you'll find the information useful in learning and refining the skills that will help you skate safely and confidently.

If you're interested in running, skiing, cycling, dance skating, racing, or simply jumping into a pair of lightweight ski boots on wheels, *In-Line Skating* will help you combine the benefits of a low-impact, highly aerobic workout with an exciting method of cross-training. You'll learn about burning calories and what muscle groups get the best workout, and find cross-training information on running, skiing, and cycling.

This book is divided into three parts. Part I provides you with what you need to know before beginning your in-line skating adventure. You'll learn what to look for and how to select your first pair of skates. Certain safety gear is an absolute must before you put on skates. You'll learn how to wear it. You'll also find out how to stretch and warm up before you skate, to avoid muscle injuries.

Part II includes photographs and illustrations with step-by-step instructions in the fundamentals of in-line skating. Drills and tips for correcting errors are included to assist you in perfecting your skills. Proper posture is the key to steady balance, and you'll see the right and wrong ways to stand. After reading *In-Line Skating*, you'll understand why stroke, glide. . .stroke, glide is better than stroke, stroke,

stroke. You'll find the answer to in-line's most frequently asked question, "How do you stop these things?" Three types of turns are taught, basic, connecting, and crossover turns. Then, after learning each individual technique, you'll discover how to put it all together into a smooth, confident style.

Part III introduces you to racing, tricks and dance, and roller hockey. We take you through the training steps for in-line racing, from completing 10Ks in less than 17 minutes, to marathons. You'll learn the street dance scene through a unique style that combines traditional figure skating jumps and spins with funky dance steps to the rhythms of today's hottest dance music. From stopping to cartwheels, we help you see the mistakes most skaters make and explain how to correct them with easy-to-understand instructions. *In-Line Skating* teaches you the fundamentals of the fast-paced and challenging game of roller hockey, and details how to form a team and league in your area.

In-Line Skating provides a solid foundation on which you can build your in-line skating skills. Whether you're training for serious athletic competition or looking for a fun workout, take time to read, learn, and practice. The time you invest in this book will pay off for many years to come.

Mark Powell and John Svensson

Acknowledgments

With sincere thanks to Ultra Wheels and Hyper Wheels for their sharing of knowledge and photographs; the staff at Gregg's Greenlake Cycles in Seattle for their support and promotion of in-line skating; Andy Barker for his knowledge and help with photography; Howie Hale for his sharing of photographs; and Kathy Durnell and Jan Witsoe, who proofread the original manuscript and questioned every detail. A special thanks to Brian Holding and Mary Fowler of Human Kinetics Publishers for their advice and support—without them this book would not have happened.

 *PART I*

BEFORE YOU SKATE

In Part I we introduce you to in-line skating and its benefits, examine skating equipment and safety equipment, and discuss what you should consider before you start skating.

Part I will not get you up and moving on your skates, but it will prepare you to be a more knowledgeable and safer participant in your new sport.

CHAPTER 1

Introduction to In-Line Skating

Welcome to the exciting world of in-line skating, one of the fastest growing sports in the world. Its growth has been fueled by athletes, recreational enthusiasts, and manufacturers alike as they've come to see that in-line skating is an inexpensive, fun, and health-promoting new activity.

Athletes from a variety of sports spurred the popularity of in-line skating with their desire to cross-train. Ice hockey players, ice speed-skaters, and cross-country and alpine skiers stimulated the growth by implementing off-season training on in-line skates. They were soon followed by runners, cyclists, and traditional roller skaters who saw the benefits of a low-impact, highly aerobic, cross-training workout.

Today in-line skating has taken on an identity of its own. No longer is it just an alternative training method for athletes from other sports; it has become a part of our culture. It is represented in television commercials for major international products and has made appearances at the Super Bowl half-time show and the opening ceremonies for the Winter Olympics.

People from all walks of life are trying in-line skating and finding it to be an inexpensive, fun, versatile recreation. And it's a great form of exercise and a healthy workout: In-line skating burns calories and tones muscles.

Two organizations help oversee the growth and management of this young sport. The International In-line Skating Association (IISA) and United States Amateur Confederation of Roller Skating (USAC/RS) certify instructors and organize such events as races, hockey matches, and artistic competitions. There is even talk among the leaders of these organizations of working toward having in-line skating become an Olympic event. (The appendix provides more details about these governing bodies.)

What's in a Name?

In-line skating is often referred to as rollerblading and the skates as rollerblades. Rollerblade, Inc. of Minneapolis, Minnesota, one of the top manufacturers of skating equipment, is often credited with developing the modern in-line skate.

Over the last several years, in-line skating has diversified and many other manufacturers have entered the market. To avoid identifying the sport with a trademarked name, in 1991 the Rollerblade In-line Skate Association changed its name to the International In-line Skating Association (IISA). Today the industry and the active participants are working to change the name of the sport to in-line skating (referring to the wheels of the skate, which are in a line).

It's Easier Than You Think

In-line skating looks hard. After all, you have to balance on a thin line of wheels. You might remember how sore your ankles got when you learned to ice skate, and looking at in-line skates can bring back those painful memories.

Fortunately, in-line skating is easier than ice skating or even traditional roller skating. This is a result of the ski-type boot made of hard plastic that is used with in-line skates. These boots provide outstanding ankle support and make it relatively easy to stand up on in-line skates.

The wheels on in-line skates are also a factor in the ease of skating. Modern urethane wheels are soft and resilient; the softness keeps the wheels from sliding out from under you while stroking or turning, and the resilience allows the wheels to roll over pebbles, cracks, and other obstacles in your path.

Another stability factor is the length of the wheel base. If you compare the length of the wheel base on roller skates and in-line skates you will find that the in-lines are at least 1 to 2 inches longer for the same size boot (see Figure 1.1, a and b). This additional length adds a great deal of front-to-back stability.

a b

Figure 1.1a,b Both skates shown are for the same size foot. The wheel base of the in-line skate (b) is 2 inches longer than the quad skate (a).

In-line skating is easier than many people think, but that doesn't mean it lacks challenges. It still takes instruction, time, and practice to become a proficient skater.

The Evolution of In-Line Skating

The concept of putting skate wheels in a line instead of side-by-side is not new. Some credit the Dutch with the invention. Others look to Louis Legrange who created a pair of in-line skates in 1849 to simulate an ice skating scene in the French opera La Prophète. The wheels were made of wood spools and did not provide traction. Therefore, turning and stopping was difficult.

Modern in-line skates grew in popularity after being developed in Minnesota in the early 1980s for a group of ice hockey players interested in training during the off-season. From that beginning the sport attracted the interest of athletes from other sports. Before long, nonathletes were skating on in-lines for the pure fun of it.

Skating is a multifaceted sport that includes recreational skaters of all ages and experience levels. The sport is developing many special interest groups, including indoor and outdoor racers, roller hockey leagues, dance and artistic skaters, and freestyle and ramp skaters. There is even a group of in-line skaters in Seattle, Washington, who meet once a week to play basketball on skates.

There are skates designed for children, adult recreation, cross-training, hockey, racing, and dancing. There are various types of wheels as well, ranging in size and hardness, depending on the application. For information on skating equipment see chapter 2.

Low-Impact Workout

One of the factors that has fueled the growth of in-line skating is the recognition that it is a low-impact yet highly aerobic workout. The stroke, recovery, and glide of in-line skating actually works more muscle groups than running, and skating is easier on the body's joints.

One of the questions asked about any aerobic exercise is, "How many calories does it burn?" The answer is not always easy because people burn calories at different rates. Most tests that measure calorie usage are done by measuring oxygen consumption and heart rate along with lactate levels and body weight.

The amount of calories you burn is related to several things:

- What physical shape you are in
- The type of exercise you do
- How hard you exert yourself
- How long you exert yourself
- Your body weight
- Your metabolism

As a reference point we will use athletes training at their highest possible sustained work load. This refers to the highest workout level that an individual can maintain for an extended period of time. According to research done by Dr. Carl Foster of the University of Wisconsin Medical School, an in-line skater working at his or her highest possible sustained work load will burn about 570 calories an hour (see

Table 1.1   Calories Expended by Athletes at Their Highest Possible Sustained Work Load

In-line skating	570 calories an hour
Running	720 calories an hour
Bicycling	570 calories an hour

Table 1.1). This is an average determined by measuring several people ranging in fitness level, sex, and weight.

Cross-Training

More and more athletes from other sports are turning to in-line skating as a cross-training workout. In-line skating is fun and exciting, and its physical demands are uniquely similar to a variety of other sports. In this section we take a close look at the benefits of cross-training on in-line skates for alpine skiing, cross-country skiing, cycling, and running.

Alpine Skiing

If you're an alpine skier who wants to hit the slopes in shape each fall you should examine the benefits of in-line skating. Whether your interests are in recreational or freestyle skating or racing, the benefits of in-line skating during the off-season are great. The combination of speed, power, and acceleration you get while carving a turn on in-line skates feels very close to skiing (see Figure 1.2, a and b). The major muscle groups of the lower body also receive a tremendous workout when you apply alpine skiing techniques to in-lines.

If your skiing interests are specific you will easily be able to discover cross-training techniques to complement your interests. Ski

a   b

Figure 1.2a,b The body posture and position of the skier and in-line skater are nearly identical while executing a turn.

racers can set up a series of cones or gates to simulate a race course. Freestyle skiers can simulate their disciplines through jumps or ballet and tricks on in-lines.

Cross-Country Skiing

Cross-country skiers will find that in-line skating is one of the closest forms of cross training available. If you compare an in-line skater with a cross-country skier, you will see that many of the motions are nearly identical (see Figure 1.3, a and b).

Figure 1.3a,b   The stroke leg and glide leg position of the cross-country skier and in-line skater are nearly identical.

Cross-country skiers can use their ski poles while on in-line skates and work out in hilly terrain. The combination of poles and hills gives a better upper body and cardiovascular workout because of the increased muscle usage and oxygen demand. But don't use ski poles in areas where there are lots of pedestrians or cyclists, especially if you don't have much experience with them.

Cycling

Cyclists will find in-line skating to be an exciting cross-training sport. It can provide speeds and racing conditions that are very similar to bike racing. There is more wheel friction resistance on in-line skates than on a bicycle, so a cross-training cyclist can build more muscle mass on skates.

The cardiovascular workout on skates is similar to that on a bicycle, but the skater will get a better workout in the same amount of time. Athletes who compare skating and cycling may belive that a skater who is gliding between strokes is resting, the same as a cyclist who is not pedaling. However, the skater must use more muscle groups to balance on one skate than the biker, who is connected to the bike at five points. This shows that the skater will get a greater cardiovascular workout, in the same amount of time, than the cyclist.

Running

Runners who have experienced physical difficulties as a result of the high-impact conditions of their sport will find relief with in-line skating. In-line skating will provide a cardiovascular workout similar to running. Runners who cross train will want to design workouts that duplicate their running workout, maintaining a similar heart rate for a similar amount of time. (When skating, you will cover more distance because of the higher speeds.)

What Are You Waiting For?

The evidence is in: In-line skating is fun, exciting, and good for you! Let's get started. In the following chapters you'll learn how to find the equipment that's right for you, including safety gear. You'll find out what to do before you start skating and where you can skate. Then, step by step (or stroke by stroke) you'll learn how to in-line skate.

After getting a handle on the basics you'll be introduced to advanced in-line skating, which will help you pursue one or more of the special niches of the sport.

So—what are you waiting for?

CHAPTER 2

Skating Equipment

Keeping up with the development of new products for in-line skating can be challenging. As the sport develops, more products are brought to market to serve the needs of the sport's participants. You'll find everything from sophisticated skates for special interest groups to shorts with hip pads sewn in to help avoid bruises when you fall.

In this chapter we look at the key pieces of in-line equipment and what you should consider before you buy. To help fuel the growth of skating, many manufacturers and retailers of in-line skates support rental and demonstration programs. Most major cities around the U.S. now have a business that offers rental or free demonstration of in-line skates and related equipment.

These rental and demonstration programs are a great way to test the sport and various types of skates; however, the skates used in rental programs are sometimes inexpensive models with low grade wheels and bearings. These characteristics are safer for the beginner, because the skates don't roll as fast, but rental skates may not give you a fair representation of the quality, or performance, of in-line skates in general.

If you're interested in testing various skates for the purpose of making a buying decision, see if the retailer has demonstration pairs of the specific models that you are considering purchasing. There can be tremendous differences in performance between models.

If you have no experience on in-line skates, read the following chapters on fundamental skating skills. Give special attention to the sections in this chapter on safety gear and the rules of the road. We cannot emphasize enough the importance of using safety gear and obeying safety rules. As a beginning skater you will be susceptible to injury. Don't take a casual attitude when getting on skates for the first time. Skate smart.

Components of In-Line Skates

In-line skates have many different components. In this section we look at each one and examine how it affects the performance of the skate and the skater.

Boots

Most boots are constructed with two pieces of molded plastic (see Figure 2.1). The lower half of the boot covers the lower portion of

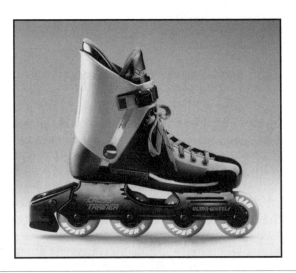

Figure 2.1   The color differences in the pieces of the boot identify the two pieces of molded plastic.

the foot, much like a tennis shoe. The upper half wraps around and supports the ankle. The upper and lower sections are connected on each side of the ankle with a hinge system that allows the ankle and boot to flex forward as the ankle would naturally flex.

The type of plastic can vary from model to model. Some plastics are more rigid and provide a stiffer boot with more ankle support, which helps you stand on the skates. Some boots have vents to help circulate air into the liner and reduce weight. Various specialty boots are constructed of leather and high-tech materials such as carbon fiber and Kevlar. These boots are primarily used for speed skating.

Tightening Systems. In-line boots utilize laces, buckles, Velcro straps, or a combination of laces and buckles to tighten and secure the boot. The most effective and popular style is a boot that laces on the lower part and buckles on the ankle for maximum support.

Height. Most in-line skate boots extend 3 to 4 inches above the ankle joint. The boots are slightly higher in the back to provide additional support. Speed-skate boots generally have a lower cut, 1 to 2 inches above the ankle joint. This lower profile gives the speed skater more flexibility but less ankle support, and is more difficult to skate in.

Liners. The liner of the in-line skate boot is similar to that of a ski boot but is not as thick or as insulating. These liners provide a great deal of support and comfort when fitted correctly, in comparison to the traditional ice skate or roller-skate boot. Most liners are constructed from high-density foam surrounded by a nylon cloth. The plastic outer shell may be designed to fit several size liners: A size 9-10 shell will fit liners in half-size increments from 9 to 10-1/2 (9, 9-1/2, 10, 10-1/2). Boots and liners usually come from the factory as a complete set.

Liners are removable, which allows a retailer to custom-fit in-line skates. This is done by building up the liner with foam pads for narrow feet or heating and stretching the plastic shells for wide feet. Custom fitting should be done only by a qualified expert; it's easy to ruin a new pair of skates if you're not familiar with the correct procedures. Many liners are washable, and you should consider this when buying if your feet sweat a lot.

Custom foot beds are also available to go inside liners. The foot bed is made from a high density foam or a stiff plastic; you heat it and then stand on it while it cools. This process creates a foot bed that is molded to your foot. Many in-line skate shops and most ski shops provide this service. Foot beds can greatly increase your skate control and comfort through providing greater arch support and support in the heel cup.

Frames

The frame is attached to the bottom of the boot and holds the wheels on the skate. On most skates the frame is a separate component that is attached to the boot with rivets or something similar. On some inexpensive skates the boot and frame are injection molded as one piece.

The largest percentage of frames are constructed from a high-impact injection molded plastic, but speed and high-performance skates are now available with frames manufactured from aluminum, carbon fiber, and titanium. These materials provide the skater with a light yet rigid frame.

Frame length is measured from the center of the front axle to the center of the rear axle. Length can vary from 10 to 16 inches depending on the size of the boot and the type of skating for which it will be used (see Figure 2.2, a and b). The most common frame length is 12 inches; this is found on most recreational and hockey skates. Longer frames are used on racing skates for greater stability, and shorter frames are used for skates with small boot sizes.

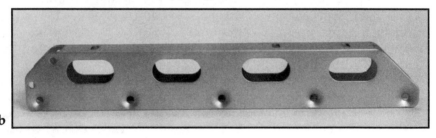

Figure 2.2a,b   These two photos show the difference between a recreational skate frame (a) and a racing skate frame (b).

Wheels

Of all the components of a pair of skates, wheels have the greatest effect on performance. As you become a more proficient skater wheel quality becomes more important. A speed skater will use a different kind of wheel on an outdoor road course than on an indoor hardwood floor. The same is true for a hockey player. The selection of wheels can dramatically affect a skate's performance.

Choosing wheels that match your skating style can seem like a complex process, and there is not always one correct choice. The following sections describe the various components and characteristics of wheels to help steer you in the right direction.

Number. The number of wheels that are mounted on an in-line frame can vary depending on the intended use of the skates, the size of the frame, and the size of the skater's foot. Standard skates have four wheels; some small skates have three wheels, and most speed skates have five. More wheels will add stability in the front-to-back direction of the skates, but will reduce the side-to-side turning ability and add weight to the skate.

Size. Wheel size is measured in millimeters (mm). The diameter of a wheel is measured from outer edge through the center of the wheel to outer edge. Most recreational skates are equipped with wheels that are 68 mm to 72 mm in diameter. These are considered small and provide a lower center of gravity, which allows the beginning skater to feel stable.

Midsize wheels are 72 mm to 76 mm in diameter, a good size if you want to skate longer distances and achieve a good aerobic workout. This size is also common for indoor racing, as it is more proficient in cornering than the larger outdoor racing wheel.

Wheels 78 mm to 82 mm in diameter are the fastest, longest lasting wheels because of their size and inertia. The larger a wheel is, the more ground it covers with each rotation. Tall wheels are less stable, side to side, because of the additional height, and they require a higher skill level (see Figure 2.3).

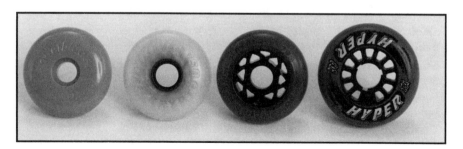

Figure 2.3 From left to right, a 70-mm wheel without a hub and a 70-mm wheel with a hub are good for recreational skates. The 72.5-mm wheel is for longer distances, and the 80-mm wheel is appropriate for racing.

Urethane. Urethane is the hard rubberlike compound that actually touches the ground. Urethane is a molded petroleum-based compound that can be made with different formulas to create wheels with varying degrees of hardness (durometer) and rebound.

Durometer. Durometer, a measurement of how hard a wheel is, is the most common indicator of a wheel's skating and performance characteristics. Durometer of in-line wheels is measured by a two-digit number that shows increasing hardness with increasing number. That is, a 78A wheel is softer than an 85A wheel. The letter A refers to the measurement scale that is used (A scale). Current in-line wheels range from 75A to 93A, with 78A and 82A being the most popular and versatile.

Skating surface, body weight, and skating abilities determine the best wheel to use. (See Table 2.1.) A soft wheel has greater traction and cornering ability, and it will absorb more of the vibration from a rough skating surface. A higher durometer wheel will be faster and more efficient on a smooth skating surface, but on a rough road it will send vibrations through the skate and be very uncomfortable on your feet and legs.

The skater's body weight is also important. A heavy skater will compress a soft wheel more and increase the "footprint" of the wheel, creating more drag and slowing the skater down. With that in mind, a heavier skater will want to skate on a harder wheel.

Table 2.1 Wheel Selection Chart

Skating surface	Body weight	Beginner	Intermediate	Advanced
Rough	Under 160 lb	78A	78A	78A
Rough	Over 160 lb	78A	78A	78A–82A
Smooth pavement	Under 160 lb	78A	78A	78A
Smooth pavement	Over 160 lb	78A	78A	78A–82A
Smooth concrete	Under 160 lb	78A	78A	78A
Smooth concrete	Over 160 lb	78A	82A–85A	82A–85A
Indoor	Under 160 lb	85A	85A	85A
Indoor	Over 160 lb	85A	85A	85A

Profile. The profile of a wheel refers to the shape of the urethane that surrounds the core. Various profiles can affect speed, cornering, and durability. A narrow wheel has the least surface contact and therefore the least resistance. A wider wheel has a larger footprint and is slower because of the greater resistance. However, the wider wheel is more stable and will last longer, because of the additional urethane.

Hub.   The hub, at the center of the wheel, separates the urethane from the bearings. Hubs are made of a stiff material that will not flex under the pressure of skating. The most common material used to make hubs is a thermoplastic nylon. In some high-performance wheels aluminum and carbon fiber are used.

In standard-size wheels, the hub may be just a thin sleeve in the center hole of the urethane that holds the bearings in place. In a large wheel the hub may be up to 50% of the diameter, and it may be spoked (see Figure 2.4). A well-designed spoked hub will help cool the ure-thane and bearings, maintain rigidity of the wheel, help tracking, and reduce overall weight.

Figure 2.4   The smaller hub is the sleeve that holds the bearings in place. A spoked hub will help cool a large wheel and keep it rigid.

Some inexpensive skates come with wheels that do not have hubs. This is one area where the manufacturer cuts back to reduce costs. These wheels do not roll as well as wheels with hubs.

Bearings.   Bearings are the ball bearings that allow the wheels of an in-line skate to spin smoothly. Modern bearings are sold in an en-closed doughnutlike metal casing that fits snugly into the center of a wheel's hub (see Figure 2.5). Each wheel has two sets of bearings, one on each side of the wheel.

There are many different types and qualities of bearings, and it can be difficult and time-consuming to sort out all of the variables that affect a bearing's performance. In general, quality skates have quali-ty bearings.

Bearings do wear out after long use. The first indication of this wear

Figure 2.5   The closed-casing bearing set as shown on the left is what modern bearings look like. With the cover removed on the right you can see the actual bearings inside the case.

is noise coming from the bearing when the wheel is spinning. These noises result from a breakdown of the grease that the bearings are packed in or because sand, rust particles, or other foreign material get into the bearing casing.

It is possible to take the bearing casing apart, clean the bearings, repack the case with grease, and replace the casing cover, but buying new bearings is not costly and is much easier. Consult your local skate shop for options on replacement bearings.

A set of bearings should last a year if you take care of them; avoid moisture, sand, and heavy dust. The outer bearing casings attract a lot of dust. Wipe these clean on a regular basis. (For instruction on bearing replacement see ''Bearing Replacement'' under ''Maintenance'' in this chapter.)

Rocker.   Rocker refers to adjusting the wheels on your in-line skates so they do not all rest flat on the ground when you're standing still (see Figure 2.6). On a four-wheel skate the center two wheels are adjusted to be taller, so that when you're standing on a flat surface the front and back wheels will be off the ground by about an eighth of an inch.

Setting your skates on a rocker will allow you to turn and spin faster, but it can cause them to be unstable when you're traveling at higher speeds or over long distances. Advanced skaters sometimes set their wheels on a rocker for hockey or for tricks and dance skating.

To set the wheels in the rocker position, remove the center two wheels (just the middle wheel on a three-wheel skate). You'll see frame spacers inserted in an oblong hole in the frame. The spacers have a hole that the axle passes through. Pop the spacers out and turn them

Figure 2.6 The center two wheels are slightly lower than the front and back wheels.

over so the axle hole is toward the bottom of the frame. Then reinstall the center wheels.

You can also shorten the wheel base through the same process. Remove the front and back wheels, and you will see that there are spacers that allow you to adjust the length of the wheel base. A longer wheel base is faster and more stable. A shorter wheel base helps you turn and spin faster.

Although these adjustments cause changes of only a fraction of an inch in the wheel base, you will be amazed at how unstable the skates feel. A short, rockered skate should only be attempted when you feel comfortable and confident on a flat skate. Even then, it will take a considerable amount of time to feel comfortable on rockered skates, but the performance benefits for the dance, trick, or hockey skater are great.

Types of In-Line Skates

As the sport of in-line skating continues to grow, more types of skates appear on the market. In this section we examine the various types of skates currently available.

Inexpensive Skates

The marketplace has become full of in-line skates priced under $100. These skates capitalize on the popularity and trendiness of the new sport. They fill a niche in the market, but it is difficult to consider them a serious piece of sporting equipment.

The manufacturers of these skates save money in the manufacturing process by using inexpensive plastics in the boot and frame. This plastic does not give the same ankle support that you will find in a higher quality skate. Remember, ankle support is one of the keys to being able to skate comfortably and safely.

Other key money-saving areas are bearings and wheels. Most of these skates have low-grade bearings and no hubs in the wheels. As a result, these skates do not roll well. This can be one of the most frustrating parts of skating on inexpensive skates; you'll stroke and stroke and not roll at all.

Skates that retail for less than $100 may be a good option for children who are still growing and want an introduction to in-line skating (see Figure 2.7). Because of the additional weight that the skates must carry, they should be avoided by adults who desire a serious recreational workout.

Figure 2.7 Most quality children's skates are available for under $100.

The investment that you make in a quality pair of skates will pay for itself many times over when compared to other sports, or membership in a health club. Quality used skates maintain a high resale value.

Recreational Skates

Most skates sold today fall into the category of recreational skates. Recreational skates provide the versatility to skate in many different fashions. Don't be fooled by the word *recreation*. These skates can be used for everything from working out to hockey.

A quality pair of recreational skates combines a stiff outer shell and comfortable inner liner with good wheels and bearings (see Figure 2.8). These skates can range in price from $150 to $250. Finding the best pair of skates for your budget and needs is a matter of testing various skates and shopping for the best combination of price and service.

Figure 2.8 Good adult recreational skates have a stiff outer shell and sell for $150 to $250.

Racing Skates

No segment of in-line skating has seen a faster development of new equipment than racing. There is a never-ending quest to design and build lighter, stiffer, and faster racing skates. Racing skates are an excellent choice for long-distance skating as well (see Figure 2.9).

These skates have several differences from recreational, dance, and hockey skates. The most obvious difference is a frame length of 13 to 15 inches, which allows the addition of an extra wheel. The longer frame provides a more stable and directed stroke and glide, but it restricts the turning radius of the skater. The frame is made of a very stiff but lightweight material such as aluminum or titanium.

It's common for racing skates to have five wheels. Some skates have four wheels, for smaller feet or for weight reduction. The wheels on racing skates are usually larger in diameter than other skates, 76 mm

Figure 2.9 Racing and long distance training skates have lower boots, longer frames, and larger wheels; they sell for $250 and up.

to 80 mm. A larger wheel has more surface area, so it rotates fewer times per mile.

The combination of a longer frame with more and larger wheels has disadvantages and advantages. The main disadvantage is weight. These extra components can add weight that will take its toll on a racer or distance skater. Manufacturers combat the weight issue by using high-tech components such as titanium, but these drive prices up.

A longer frame is more difficult to push out and away from your body during a stroke. Therefore, acceleration and climbing hills tends to be slower on a long frame. The advantage of these skates becomes apparent once you get them up to a pace or racing speed. The stability and inertia of a long frame and large wheels will have a significant positive effect on your ability to maintain a high speed with the least amount of physical effort.

You will also find differences between a racing boot and other skates. The racing boot is cut lower around the ankle and preferably constructed of a light-weight yet stiff material. Some leather boots are available—they are popular with serious racers but they are expensive and do not provide the level of ankle support found in plastic boots.

A quality pair of in-line racing skates will cost between $350 and $600. Most skaters will find that skates in the $400 price range will meet their needs. Anticipate spending slightly more money per year on wheels and bearings than for recreational skates. More miles skated equals more frequent replacement of wheels and bearings.

Dance Skates

In-line skates designed specifically for dance and trick skating are still in the development stage. In-line skates have not evolved as far as ice skates and roller skates, where you will find skates with special features for the creative disciplines.

Now that the United States Amateur Confederation of Roller Skating has decided to allow in-line skates into their competitions (see the appendix), it will be interesting to see what kind of impact they have on the artistic competitions. As the interest in this type of skating grows, more products will be developed to fill the demand.

If you want to get involved in the dance or trick aspects of in-line skating there are some key features you should look for in a skate. The skates should have a very stiff outer shell and frame. Because of the turns and jumps you may be doing, you will put a lot of lateral (sideways) pressure on the skates. If the skate is constructed of lighter weight material it will flex under this lateral pressure. This flex can cause a lack of ankle support and loss of control if the frame bends.

Smaller diameter wheels are also important on dance and trick skates; they lower your center of gravity and make you more stable. Wheel hardness will vary depending on the skating surface. Use a harder wheel on a smooth surface and softer wheel on a rough surface.

You should buy skates that have frames that allow you to rocker the wheels. Although you may not do this right away, you'll want to have the option available as your skill level increases (for information on rockering, see pages 18-19).

Hockey Skates

Some in-line skate manufacturers are now offering skates specifically designed for roller hockey (see Figure 2.10). These skates have a relatively short frame, and you can rocker the wheels; short, rockered skates allow you to turn and spin quickly. The boot and frame of the skates are made of heavier than normal plastics, so they'll stand up to the abuses of hockey.

There are now wheels specifically designed for hockey players as well. Hockey wheels are small, 70 mm in diameter, to lower the skater's center of gravity. They also are wide profile wheels; the skate can be turned sharply without sliding out from under the skater.

Skate Maintenance

In-line skates are relatively low maintenance, and that is one of the inviting aspects of the sport. You can put on your skates and get a

Figure 2.10 Hockey skates have short frames, small wheels, and strong boots. Prices are similar to recreational skates.

good workout without a lot of set-up or clean-up time. However, your skates will need occasional attention.

Tools

It's a great idea to put together a skate repair kit that you can carry in your skate bag. A list of recommended tools appears in Table 2.2. Be sure to choose components and tools that fit your particular model of skate since different skates have different sizes of wheels, wrenches, etc. Your local skate shop can help you with the selection of components and tools.

Table 2.2 Recommended Tools for Skate Maintenance

Minimum requirements	Suggested additions
2 Allen wrenches	Bearings
1 box wrench or socket wrench (socket preferred)	Washers (if used on your axles)
	Spare axle
1 bearing removal tool	Replacement brake
1 screw driver (for brake replacement; check for Phillips or regular)	Spare wheels
	Frame spacers
Cleaning rags	Bearing spacers
	Extra laces

Wheel Rotation or Replacement

The most common maintenance activity you will be performing on your skates is rotation of the wheels. Wheels wear down while skating; to get the maximum mileage, proper rotation is necessary. The inside edges of the wheels usually wear down more quickly than the outside, due to the natural pushing motion of skating.

Wheels may also wear down more in the front or in the rear, depending on whether you push off with your toe or heel. Every skater strokes differently, so everyone creates a different wear pattern on their wheels.

Take a good look at your wheels to see the wear patterns. If the wheels are starting to look worn at an angle along the inside edges, it's time to rotate them (see Figure 2.11). Rotation is changing the position of the wheels on the frame and turning the wheels over so the inside edges become the outside edges.

Figure 2.11 On the left is a new wheel. On the right is a wheel that's heavily worn; it should have been rotated before the wear became so extreme.

We refer to the front wheel as position number 1, the second wheel as position number 2, and so on. (See Figure 2.12.)

To rotate your wheels, follow these directions:

Wheel in position		*Move to position*
1	to	3
2	to	4
3	to	1
4	to	2

Figure 2.12 The diagram shows the pattern for rotating wheels.

Note that you are moving the front and back wheels to the center positions. With three- and five-wheel skates move the most worn wheels to the positions that show the least amount of wear.

The axle bolts have a flush mount. The flush part of the bolt *must* face the inside of the skate (see Figure 2.13). As you push your skate out when stroking, the inside edge of the frame comes close to the ground. If you replace the axle bolt with the nut end on the inside

Figure 2.13 When replacing axle bolts, be sure that the flat bolt head faces the inside of the skate frame.

it is easy to hit the bolt when stroking. This can be dangerous, as the bolt and nut may catch on the ground or slide out from under you when the metal contacts the ground.

If your wheels are worn down and need to be replaced, follow these instructions and those in "Bearing Replacement."

To remove and replace the wheels follow these steps:

1. Brace the skate between your legs with the wheels up (see Figure 2.14). Utilizing the appropriate Allen, box, or socket wrench, loosen and remove each axle.

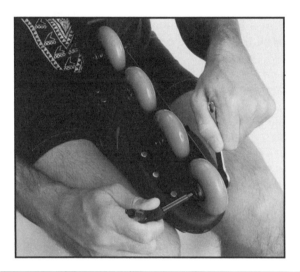

Figure 2.14 Position and tools for working on skates.

2. Rotate the wheels to the appropriate position. As you remove the wheels, wipe all dust and grime from the bearing casings and the frame spacers. Remember to flip the wheels so the worn side is now facing out. (There is no need to rotate wheels from one skate to the other unless you have a dramatic wear difference between skates.)

3. Realign the wheels with the axle holes, insert the axle bolt, and screw the nut on (nut facing the outside edge of the frame). Tighten each axle and nut until snug.

4. Spin each wheel to make sure it spins freely. If a wheel does not spin well, loosen the axle nut slightly and try to spin it again. If a wheel makes noise when it spins, it may be time to replace the bearings. Identify which bearing is making the noise and replace it (see "Bearing Replacement").

Note that the axle bolt for the wheel closest to the brake is longer than the other axle bolts. The part of the frame that holds the brake in place is secured with the back axle. Be sure to replace this bolt in its original position.

Bearing Replacement

To replace the bearings follow these steps:

1. Remove the wheels as noted in the previous section.

2. Place the bearing tool into the axle hole and press the bearing that's on the opposite side of the wheel out of the wheel hub. Turn the wheel over and remove the nylon bearing spacer. The bearing spacer provides a lining for the axle to pass through and keeps the bearings from sliding into the center of the hub (see Figures 2.15 and 2.16).

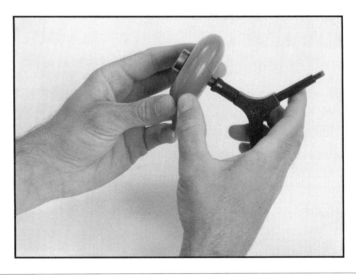

Figure 2.15 Use a bearing tool to press the bearings out of the wheel hub.

3. Put the bearing tool through the hub from the back and press the second bearing out.

4. With a damp cloth, remove all dirt and grime from the inside of the wheel hub. If the inside of the bearing spacers are dirty, use a cotton swab to remove the dirt. If the bearing spacers show wear, replace them.

5. Insert a new bearing casing into one side of the wheel hub. Be sure to press the bearing case into the hub until it is flush with the edge of the hub. Turn the wheel over and insert the bearing spacer. Align the second bearing case with the spacer and press it into the

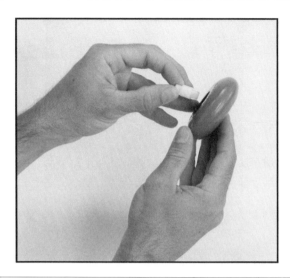

Figure 2.16 Turn the wheel over, remove the nylon bearing spacer, and press the second bearing out from the back side of the bearing.

hub. Be careful to align properly so you don't press the side of the bearing casing into the ball bearings with the end of the spacer.

6. Replace the wheels according to the instructions given on page 27.

If you are installing new wheels follow the same instructions, but insert your current bearings into the new wheels.

Brake Replacement

Brakes wear out and should be replaced when you have to lift your toe too high to be stable when stopping, or when the bolt holding the brake in place begins to rub the ground. Your local skate shop can provide you with a replacement brake for your model of skates.

Brakes have a through bolt that can be loosened with either a screw driver, Allen wrench, or socket wrench depending on the type of brake. The replacement of the brake is straightforward. Loosen the bolt, remove the brake, and attach the new brake (see Figure 2.17).

Upgrading Your Skates

If you have previously purchased a pair of inexpensive in-line skates and have decided that the performance is unsatisfactory, you do not have to start from scratch. Most of the important components on your skates can be upgraded for less than the cost of a new pair of skates.

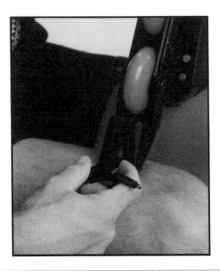

Figure 2.17   Different brakes have different systems for securing them. Most are easily replaced.

The first item to consider replacing is bearings. Bearings can have the single biggest effect on the performance of inexpensive skates. Check with your local skate shop for a quality set of bearings. You do not have to buy a high-performance set of bearings to see an increase in the performance.

While you're at the skate shop, check into upgrading your wheels. Refer to the section on wheels in this chapter and consult with experts at the shop about the type of wheels you should select. Bearings and wheels can be purchased at separate times. If money is a consideration, get the bearings first.

Many inexpensive skates do not provide adequate ankle support, especially for adult skaters. If you have trouble standing up straight on your in-line skates, chances are good that you don't have the necessary ankle support. To correct this problem ask your skate shop about ankle straps (see Figure 2.18). These are 1/2- to 1-1/2-inch-wide straps of nylon and Velcro that go around the outside of the skate boot at the ankle, and can be tightened to provide more ankle support. There are several manufacturers of these straps; if your local shop does not have them in stock they can be ordered.

Safety Gear

Safety is one of the most important issues facing in-line skating today. Take the time and money to invest in, and use, the appropriate safety gear.

Figure 2.18 An ankle support strap will help increase the rigidity of ankle cuffs on skates.

When skating, and when looking at the pictures in this book, you will see some skaters who are not wearing a full complement of safety gear. An experienced skater, skating without safety gear, is taking a calculated risk based on his or her skills and the skating conditions.

For example, it would be unusual to see bicycle racers with knee pads on, but they always wear helmets. They have made a decision to risk scrapes and bruises, but not risk a skull fracture. The same is true for racers on in-line skates; they all wear helmets, but the number who wear pads is relatively small. This personal decision becomes one of skills versus risks.

It would be foolish for an inexperienced skater to practice, or learn to skate, without a full complement of safety gear on. The following is a list of suggested safety gear:

1. **Helmet**—Few helmets are made specifically for in-line skating. Check the selection at your local bike shop. Select a helmet that is SNEL or ANSI safety-certified and provides a snug, comfortable fit.

2. **Wrist Guards**—The most common injuries from skating accidents are sprained or broken wrists. This is a result of the skater putting out a hand to break a fall. It does not take much speed to injure a wrist. Wear wrist guards at all times! The plastic brace is worn on the inside of the wrist so it crosses the palm of the hand (see Figure 2.19).

3. **Knee Pads and Elbow Pads**—Knee and elbow pads are designed to help prevent scrapes and bruises. Use only the style that has a hard plastic shield over the pad (see Figure 2.20). Do not use cloth-covered pads from other sports such as volleyball. If you fall, these pads will not slide across cement or asphalt; they catch and then slide up the

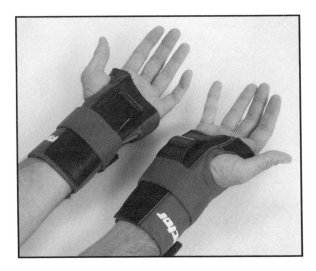

Figure 2.19 Wrist guards properly worn will help prevent injuries. The plastic bar should cover the bottom of the wrist and palm of the hand. There are right and left wrist guards; they are not interchangeable.

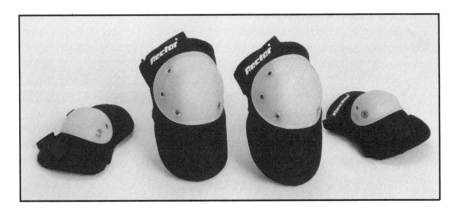

Figure 2.20 Plastic-covered knee pads and elbow pads are important pieces of safety equipment.

leg or arm, exposing the joint they should be protecting. The plastic-covered pads slide across the surface.

The money you spend on safety gear is an investment. If you can't afford safety gear, you can't afford to skate! Skate smart! For information on extra safety gear for roller hockey, see chapter 11.

Carrying Bag

It's a good idea to have a large bag to carry all of your skate gear. Many manufacturers make bags specifically for carrying skate gear; check with your local skate shop on the options.

Another spot to check is a military surplus store. Look for a bag with one large compartment for your skates and several smaller compartments for your safety gear, tools, parts, and some extra skate clothes, including socks. You might want to carry your skating bag in your car, so you can take advantage of any available skating time.

 **CHAPTER 3**

Before You Start

Before you get started in in-line skating it's important to take a few more things into consideration. In this chapter we look at some important preskate activities.

Skate Smart

The in-line skate manufacturers and IISA sponsor a public awareness campaign called Skate Smart. They distribute posters to skate shops and run advertisements in magazines to increase safety awareness in skaters. Their message is this: "Skate smart. Lead by example. Honor the rules of the road. Be especially watchful for others. Wear protective gear and always skate under control. Thanks for making this a great sport."

Rules of the Road

1. Wear safety equipment: wrist guards, knee and elbow pads, and helmet.
2. Stay alert and be courteous at all times.
3. Control your speed.
4. Skate on the right side of paths, trails, and sidewalks.
5. Overtake other pedestrians, cyclists, and skaters on the left. Use extra caution; announce your intentions by saying, ''passing on your left.'' Pass only when it is safe, and only when you have enough room for both you and the person you're passing to be at the full extension position of your strokes.
6. Be aware of changes in trail conditions due to traffic, weather conditions, and such hazards as water, potholes, or storm debris. When in doubt, slow down. Do not skate on wet or oily surfaces.
7. Obey all traffic regulations. When on skates you have the same obligations as a moving vehicle.
8. Stay out of areas with heavy automobile traffic.
9. Always yield to pedestrians.
10. Before using any trail, achieve a basic skill level, including the ability to turn, control speed, brake down hills, and recognize and avoid skating obstacles.

Keeping In-Line Skating Legal

In-line skating's phenomenal growth has led to a dramatic increase in skaters on roads, paths, and in parks all across the United States. This increase, and the perception of danger by the nonskating public, has lead to many cities regulating, or even forbidding, skaters access to public parks, trails, and roads.

The IISA has successfully fought against these regulations in many cities, but the issue of keeping skating legal across the United States is one that will continue to be debated.

In *InLine Magazine*, December/January 1992, Dave Cooper (a member of the IISA steering committee) introduced 10 steps that skaters can take to head off regulations in their communities:

1. Skate smart. Build the image of the in-line skater as a safety-conscious individual.
2. Align with the bicyclist. Bikers are pursuing a ''legitimate'' sport; let this rub off.
3. Sponsor family days. Any time Grandma and the kids do something, it's cute.

4. Skate with community leaders. They all want to "try it." Educate them.
5. Offer the law enforcement community help.
6. Sponsor safety clinics.
7. Attend regulatory meetings (traffic, city, school). Wear your good clothes.
8. Sponsor a school program. Get the educators behind the in-line movement.
9. Visit the rental shop. Help them have safe customers.
10. Police yourself. Remember that the sport of in-line skating is cool, fun, and can be quite wacky, but as role models for the beginner, we all have a responsibility to execute our more dangerous maneuvers out of view of the public. By all means push the sport and make the most of your skate, but also skate smart, skate polite, and, when appropriate, skate stealth!

Where to Skate—Outdoors

Selecting a good place to skate depends on the type of skating you're interested in and your skill level. As a beginner, you should look for a large, smooth, flat surface with as few obstructions as possible. Two good locations are the blacktop of a schoolyard or a large paved parking lot. These should be used only when they are not being utilized for their normal purpose, and you should always obey no-trespassing rules.

As your skill level increases you will want to look for similar wide-open surfaces with a slight downgrade so you can practice connecting turns while coasting downhill.

When you become proficient in stroking, turning, stopping, and avoiding obstacles, your choice of skating locations increases. Bicycle trails are a great place to get a scenic and long-distance workout. To learn more about trail systems contact the parks department in your community.

If you have a large bicycling community in your area, check with a local bike shop and find out if any "criterium style" bike racing goes on in the area. If so, find out where their races and practices take place. Criterium bike racing is similar to in-line skate racing, and their training grounds may be a good training area for in-line skating.

Wherever you decide to skate, obey the rules of the road, skate smart, and respect the rights of private property owners. You and those you skate with have a role in keeping skating safe and legal in your community.

Where to Skate—Indoors

The obvious place to in-line skate indoors is the traditional roller-skating rink. Many roller-rink operators around the United States have been hesitant to allow in-line skaters to use their rinks. Many fear their wood floors will be scratched or worry that this new sport will threaten their traditional business. To overcome the equipment questions, cover the nut end of your axle bolts with duct tape and use a nonscuff brake to avoid black marks on the floors. Check with your local skate shop for a nonscuff brake; for a short-term solution, cover your brake with duct tape.

Now that the United States Amateur Confederation of Roller Skating has legalized in-line skates for their indoor competitions (see the appendix) most rink operators are lifting their restrictions. If you have a rink operator in your community who still won't allow in-lines, contact USAC/RS and get a copy of the rule changes; then ask the rink owner for a meeting. Give information about the growth of in-line skating, and changes in USAC/RS rules. Explain to the owner that he or she is losing money, from admission fees and from the possibility of selling in-line equipment in their pro shop. Rink operators are businesspeople; if they realize the level of potential revenue that they are missing by restricting in-line skates, they may change their minds. Be sure to handle yourself in a professional manner; appeal to their business sense.

Another possibility for indoor skating is a school gymnasium. Again, this may take some work to get approved. Follow the guidelines for protecting wood floors.

Contact the school district and find out if they have a continuing education program. These are non-credit classes usually taught by people in the community, and are conducted on evenings and weekends. Contact the director of the continuing education program. They are always on the lookout for new, interesting classes that will attract people from the community. Then contact the manager of the local skate rental and sales shop and ask for a meeting.

Here is the proposal: One night a week the school sponsors an introductory in-line skating class for the community. The school advertises, promotes, and registers participants, and provides the facility. The skate shop provides free skates, safety equipment, and one or two instructors if needed. The skate shop gets positive exposure to new skaters and will undoubtedly sell some skates. You coordinate the proposal and get a great indoor spot to skate!

Physical Considerations

In-line skating is a strenuous physical activity. If you have any health problems, consult your doctor before starting.

Stretching

Before you put your skates on it is important to spend time stretching and warming up. A 5- to 10-minute warmup will go a long way toward reducing the risk of injury. Warming up will also help you feel more relaxed and confident while you skate.

Begin your preskate activities by walking, jogging, or even skating slowly for 5 to 10 minutes. The objective is to get your blood circulating throughout your muscles before you begin stretching them. Once you have warmed up your muscles, you can begin the stretches outlined below.

These eight stretching exercises will help loosen and warm up the primary muscle groups that are used while in-line skating. Each stretch should be executed slowly, without bouncing or jerking the muscle. Start each stretch by slowly applying pressure for 20 to 30 seconds. It takes at least this long to properly stretch any muscle that is not already warmed up.

Proper breathing during the stretches is important to help increase your lung capacity and assist in being loose and relaxed. While each stretch is being executed, relax the rest of your body and exhale slowly.

1. Neck

Rotate head in a circular motion for 30 seconds. Use each arm to tilt head toward shoulder and hold for 20 seconds, once each side.

2. Quadriceps (thighs)

Stand facing a wall with one hand against it for balance. Bend one leg at the knee and raise the foot up behind the buttocks. Hold the raised foot with your free hand and pull it toward your buttock. Hold the stretch. Repeat with the other leg.

3. Back/Hamstring

Sit on the ground with one leg out straight. Bring the other leg in so the heel is near the groin. Bend forward and grasp the foot of the straight leg. Bend forward at the waist toward the outstretched leg. Hold the stretch. Repeat with the other leg.

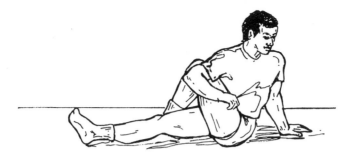

4. Buttocks/Hips

Sit on the ground with one leg extended. Cross the other leg over, placing the foot flat on the ground near the knee. Twist the upper body in the direction of the raised leg and balance on one hand. Place the other arm on the side of the raised knee, applying pressure to the knee. Hold the stretch. Repeat with the other leg.

5. Groin/Hamstring

Sit on the ground with both legs out and spread as far as comfortably possible. Lean forward at the waist, lower the upper body toward one leg. Hold the stretch. Repeat the stretch to the other leg.

6. Ankle/Calf

Sit with one leg out straight. Cross the other leg over and hold it at the ankle and the top of the foot. Pull the foot toward your body while exhaling. Hold the stretch. Repeat with the other leg.

7. Lower Back

Lie on your back. Raise your knees up so your heels are near your buttocks. Bending at the waist, raise your legs up, bringing your knees close to your chest. Leave head flat against ground. Hold stretch.

8. Duck Walk

With your skates on, walk for 3 minutes with your toes pointing out as far as comfortably possible.

PART II

GETTING STARTED

You may be learning to in-line skate purely for fun and exercise, or you may want to learn to race, dance, or play hockey. Whatever your motivation, the fundamentals are the foundation on which you will build the skills that will allow you to skate safely and skillfully.

It's not difficult to simply don a pair of in-line skates and safety gear and take a few laps around a park. But learning by your own trial and error is not the smartest way. Without some instruction, your learning will be slower and it's difficult to identify and correct mistakes.

In the following chapters we'll analyze and dissect the basics of in-line skating: posture, stroke and glide, stopping, turns, and putting it all together. You will learn the proper execution of each skill along with common mistakes. This knowledge of errors will help you see and understand the subtle differences between the right way and the wrong way to lay a solid foundation.

To continue building on your foundation, nothing will replace practice and time on your skates. Study the following chapters, then give yourself time to practice and learn. Skate smart! Wear your safety gear and follow the rules of the road.

CHAPTER 4

Posture

Posture is the most important element of the in-line skating foundation. Most falls by beginning skaters come as your skates zoom out in front of you while you fall backwards onto your rear end. Not a very exciting introduction to an exciting sport! Without exception, these falls can be attributed to improper posture.

Elements of Posture

Posture is the positioning of your torso, arms, legs, and skates so they are balanced and centered. With right posture your body stays centered over your skates even as the skating environment, conditions, and speeds change.

Proper posture starts with your eyes: Keep your head up and eyes watching where you're going, not looking down at your skates. Always be aware of where you're going and what obstacles may be ahead. Both shoulders and hips should be upright and squared to the direction you are moving.

Most important to proper posture are your legs and skates. Your legs should be bent at the knee and forward at the ankle so you can feel your ankle pressing against the tongue of your boot. By bending your ankles and knees forward, you put your weight over the balls of your feet.

Think of your legs as shock absorbers. As you skate you will encounter changes in speed and terrain, inclines and declines, bumps and curbs. Your knees and ankles are the joints that allow your legs to flex and absorb the change in conditions.

Stance

Stance, or the position of your skates on the ground, is measured in width and length. Width is the side-to-side distance between your skates, and length is the front-to-back separation.

Width

Position your skates directly under your hips, about 10 to 12 inches apart (see Figure 4.1). The width of your stance will vary if you are stroking (see chapter 5). It is common to see new in-line skaters using a very wide stance, but this undermines their ability to make fluid and stable strokes, turns, and stops.

Figure 4.1 Width of stance should be 10 to 12 inches apart.

Length

The length of your stance is one of the most important fundamentals of in-line skating. Adding length to your stance has a dramatic affect (see Figure 4.2). While standing or coasting, you're much more stable when you use a long stance than when you use a square stance. A long stance makes it more difficult to fall forward or backward. It's easier for your legs to act as shock absorbers when one leg absorbs shocks first and then the other.

Figure 4.2   A longer stance will add considerably to front-to-back stability.

Imagine a bicycle with two wheels side by side, instead of one in front of the other. Trying to stay balanced on the side-by-side bike would be like riding a two-wheeled unicycle. However, as soon as you move one of the wheels even slightly ahead of the other, your stability dramatically increases. The same is true on in-line skates; as you increase the length of your wheel base, you increase your stability.

The length of your stance can vary depending on the skating conditions. When you are standing still one skate may be 3 to 4 inches in front of the other. When coasting, the heel of your front skate will be approximately even with the toe of your back skate. When executing a high speed turn there may be as much as two skate lengths between skates.

Weight Distribution

Your weight should stay evenly distributed between your skates, even when they are separated. As your skill level increases you'll learn to shift your weight from one skate to another as you execute such maneuvers as strokes, turns, and stops. These techniques will be discussed in later chapters.

Relax

It's important to stay relaxed while skating. As you read and learn about posture and positioning, remember that these positions are not absolutely fixed. Your body is constantly changing, depending on the terrain, your speed, and the maneuver you're executing.

If you skate with a stiff body, you'll be unable to absorb shocks or adjust to changing conditions. Stiffness is a result of trying too hard to control your skates, and it can result in rapidly fatigued muscles.

In-line skating, like skiing, is a sport of technique more than strength. Don't force it. Practice and relax.

DRILLS

Weight Forward

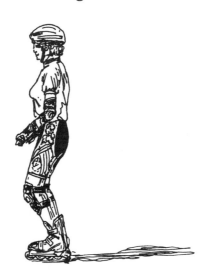

Objective: Feel your weight over the balls of your feet.

Location: Nonrolling surface (grass or carpet).

1. Look forward. Focus on an object 15 to 20 feet in front of you.
2. Square your shoulders to the direction you're facing.

3. Put your arms in front of you, at a 45-degree angle from your shoulders.
4. Keep your hips erect; don't bend forward
5. Bend your knees slightly; stay relaxed.
6. Bend your ankles forward. Feel the tongue of the boot against your ankle.
7. Keep your skates no more than 12 inches apart (width of stance).

Deep Knee Bends

Objective: Simulating legs as shock absorbers, maintaining balance while changing position.

Location: Nonrolling surface (grass or carpet).

1. Maintain the same position as described in weight forward.
2. Bend your ankles forward.
3. Compress (bend) your knees.
4. Lower your hips, but don't bend forward at the hip.
5. Move up and down several times.

Length Stance

Objective: Move skates into extended length stance, either skate forward.

Location: Nonrolling surface (grass or carpet).

1. Maintain the same position as described in the weight-forward drill (width of stance no more than 12 inches).
2. Slide right skate forward one skate length; right knee will straighten slightly.
3. Slide left skate back one skate length; left knee will compress slightly.
4. Slide the right skate back and the left skate forward at the same time (alternate positions).
5. Practice alternating forward skates several times.

Common Mistakes and Correcting Them

1. Skates feel like they are going to zoom out in front of you: Weight is too far back, knees and ankles are not bent forward. Feel your ankles press against the tongue of the boot. Move your skates into a stance with extended length for more stability.
2. Trouble maintaining side-to-side balance while alternating forward skate: The width of your stance may be too close; skates should pass each other 8 to 12 inches apart. You also may be standing too straight-legged: keep knees and ankles bent forward while allowing them to flex with changes in position, relax.

REMEMBER

1. Keep weight forward over balls of feet.
2. Practice deep knee bends with skates on.
3. Alternate forward skate in extended length stance.

 **CHAPTER 5**

Stroke, Glide . . . Stroke, Glide

Understanding the stroke-glide style of skating versus the stroke, stroke, stroke style is important. In-line skating requires motion, which will be created either by you or by gravity. You push with one leg at a time; the other leg supports your body and glides along the skating surface.

Creating Motion and Momentum

The outward stroke of your skate and the following glide will create your forward motion and momentum. A properly executed stroke and glide combination creates the maximum amount of forward motion while using the least amount of energy. We refer to this as an efficient stroke.

You may not be concerned with the efficiency of your stroke at this stage of learning, but this is the foundation of your skating; the techniques you learn now will stay with you as long as you skate.

Stroke and glide means that one skate is stroking outward and slightly back, pushing you forward. The other skate is gliding, or coasting, and taking advantage of that forward momentum.

Body Position

In chapter 4, you learned the importance of staying balanced and centered over your skates. While stroking, your body weight will shift and be centered on the glide skate.

Imagine a vertical line dividing your upper body in half. Extend the line down; it should be perfectly aligned with the center of your skate (see Figure 5.1). This will require you to move your body over the glide skate.

Figure 5.1 The vertical line shows proper body position—the upper body and knee are aligned above the skate wheels.

Stay relaxed and bend your knees and ankles forward. Keep your shoulders and hips square to your direction of motion. Keep your head up, and watch where you're going.

Stroke

The stroke is the extension of your leg; this pushes your body forward, creating motion (see Figure 5.2). The stroke extends out and away from your body at approximately a 45-degree angle to the side.

Figure 5.2 The stroke will extend a 45-degree angle behind your body.

As you begin to take a stroke, shift your body weight to the non-stroke (glide) skate. Your stroke creates motion, and you will then coast on the glide skate. As you glide, bring the stroke skate back in and underneath your body. Then shift your weight to the stroke skate, which now becomes the glide skate, and stroke with the previous glide skate.

Glide Stance

There will be times—coasting down a hill, for instance—when you will not need to stroke (see Figure 5.3). You should always coast with an extended length stance. One skate should always be out in front of the other, as taught in chapter 4. An extended length stance will greatly increase your stability.

The width of your stance will remain 8 to 12 inches, as described in chapter 4. Widening your stance will not allow you to fully extend your stroke skate, because you will not be able to shift all of your weight onto the glide skate.

Figure 5.3   Always coast with an extended length stance for more stability.

Stroke, Glide—Not Stroke, Stroke

The glide portion of skating is as important as the stroke. Many beginning skaters create motion with a series of quick short strokes, but they do not take advantage of the momentum they have created. After you have extended your leg in a stroke, you can maximize the glide by slowly returning the stroke leg under your body.

DRILLS

Skate and Body Positioning

(See Figure 5.1)

Objective: Balance on glide skate while extending stroke skate.

Location: Nonrolling surface (grass or carpet).

1. Focus on an object 15 to 20 feet in front of you.
2. Square your shoulders to the direction you're facing.
3. Bend forward with the left knee and ankle.
4. Shift your body weight to your left leg.
5. Fully extend your right leg away and to the side of your body at a 45-degree angle.
6. Maintain balance with your body weight over your left leg.
7. Repeat steps 3 through 6, balancing over your right leg, and extend stroke with your left leg.

8. Alternate stroke and glide legs several times until balance is comfortable on both.

Creating Motion

(See Figure 5.2)

Objective: Practice stroke and glide.

Location: Flat, open, hard, rolling surface.

1. Put on all safety gear as described in chapter 2.
2. Stay relaxed and keep your knees and ankles bent forward.
3. Shift your body weight over your left leg.
4. Stroke with your right leg, glide on the left skate.
5. Bring your right leg underneath your body.
6. Shift your body weight to your right leg.
7. Stroke with your left leg, glide on the right skate.
8. Return your left leg underneath your body.
9. Coast to a stop while balanced on both skates.

Coasting: Extended Length Stance

(See Figure 5.3)

Objective: Coasting in the extended length stance, either skate forward.

Location: Flat, open, hard, rolling surface.

1. Execute three consecutive stroke and glide combinations.
2. Begin coasting on both skates.
3. Move your right skate slightly in front of your body.
4. Move your left skate slightly behind your body.
5. Coast 10 to 20 feet in the extended length stance.
6. Execute the same maneuvers, coasting with the left skate forward.
7. Execute the same maneuvers, alternating forward skates while coasting.
8. Practice until you're confident coasting with either skate forward.

Common Mistakes and Correcting Them

1. Unable to balance body over glide skate: Your stance is too wide and consequently you cannot bring the glide skate underneath your body enough to be centered over the skate (see Figure 5.4). Practice standing on a nonrolling surface and balancing on one skate while lifting the other skate one inch off the ground.

Figure 5.4 A stance that is too wide will reduce efficiency, because you cannot balance and glide on one skate.

2. Unbalanced, falling forward or backward while coasting: You're not utilizing the extended length stance. Always coast with one skate slightly ahead of the other. Review "Length" on page 49.
3. Unbalanced, stiff, or tight posture: Relax and maintain the forward bend in your knees and ankles. Keep body weight over the balls of your feet, even when gliding on one skate.

REMEMBER

1. Stroke with right leg, balance and glide on left skate.
2. Stroke with left leg, balance and glide on right skate.
3. Consecutive stroke and glide alternating legs.
4. Stroke and glide—coast with extended length stance, either skate forward.

CHAPTER 6

Stopping

The most common question asked by new in-line skaters is "How do I stop?" It's easy to see maneuvers that are similar on in-line skates and in other sports such as roller skating, ice skating, and skiing. Stopping on in-lines is the exception to those similarities. But stopping is not hard, it's just different, and it requires practice to gain confidence and proficiency.

Brake Stop

On most in-line skates the brake is located behind the back wheel of the right skate. Some in-line skates have brakes on both skates and some more advanced skates do not have a brake at all. On skates with the brake on one side, the brake can be moved to either skate allowing you to use your stronger leg.

If you've roller skated and are accustomed to rolling up onto a toe stop, you'll want to relearn quickly. Rolling up on your toes on in-line skates will send you tumbling onto your chin!

We will assume in our instructions that your brake is on the back of your right skate.

Body Position

The proper stopping position on in-line skates is an extension of the extended length stance (see Figure 6.1). In the extended length stance, with the right skate forward, lift the right toe until the brake pad contacts the ground and creates friction to slow you down.

Figure 6.1   From the extended length stance with the brake skate forward, lift your toe to apply the brake.

If you're coasting in the extended length stance you will shift most of your weight to your left skate and drop your rear end toward the ground. This is the same motion as sitting down in a chair. Your arms should be up and out in front of your body. This will help offset the forward momentum of your upper body as your skates slow down.

Dropping your rear end will provide more leverage against the brake and allow you to stop faster. The drop will require bending the left knee. As you lift the right skate's toe to apply the brake, the right knee will straighten.

Figure 6.2 When applying the brake from a higher speed you must lower your body.

As you gain confidence you'll be able to stop from higher speeds. The faster you're going, the more pressure you'll have to apply to the brake (see Figure 6.2).

Stopping on Hills

The key to stopping on hills is maintaining control. New in-line skaters are often surprised at how fast in-line skates can accelerate on hills. Anticipate your potential acceleration and start applying the brakes early to keep your speed down.

T-Stop

The brake stop is the most common stop, but there are some conditions that will require an alternate. The most common alternative is the T-stop (see Figure 6.3), in which the position of the skates creates a T.

The T-stop is executed by dragging one skate behind the other at a 90-degree angle to your direction of motion. Applying pressure to the inside edges of the wheels of the skate that is being dragged will slow you down.

Figure 6.3   The drag skate is at a 90-degree angle to the direction of movement when you execute a T-stop.

When skating you will come across situations that force you to stop quickly, perhaps to avoid another person or an obstacle. Knowing how to execute two different types of stops will help you stop in any situation. In the regular stop your skate moves out in front of you; in the T-stop the skate moves behind you. These differences give you more options. It takes time and practice to master these techniques, but keep practicing both and you'll aquire that mastery.

The disadvantage to the T-stop is wearing out wheels. You are using the inside edges of the wheels as a brake, greatly increasing wear. You can reduce this by allowing yourself more space to slow down and not putting as much pressure on the wheels.

Most skaters favor dragging one skate more than the other. If you feel more comfortable balancing on your right skate and dragging your left, practice the T-stop that way. Practice it with increasing speed until you feel comfortable and confident executing the stop.

Advanced Stops

The more advanced ways of stopping on in-line skates should be used only by skaters with a high degree of skill.

Y-Stop

When executing a Y-stop you set one skate slightly behind you at a 45-degree angle (see Figure 6.4). This will cause you to turn sharply. The friction of a sharp turn will cause you to slow down.

Figure 6.4 In the Y-stop, set the skate at a 45-degree angle to the direction of travel; this will cause you to spin or rotate to a stop.

Hockey Stop

Hockey stops are more difficult on in-line skates than on ice skates. On ice, a hockey stop is a quick, sharp turn that causes the skate blades to slide sideways. On in-line skates the wheels are sticky, and the skating surface is rougher than ice. The combination of wheels and

Figure 6.5 In the hockey stop lean into a sharp turn, making the wheels breakaway, and slide.

surface creates more traction and makes it difficult for the wheels to break away and slide sideways.

Hockey stops (see Figure 6.5) can be executed on in-line skates, but it takes a high level of skill and speed to get the skates to break away and slide. This is the least common way to stop on in-line skates and should be attempted only by very skilled skaters.

Power Slide

The power slide is a stop that requires you to turn until you are skating backward and then extend one skate in your direction of motion (see Figure 6.6). The extended skate slides against the ground to create friction. This stop requires you to balance your body weight on the skate that remains under your body.

Figure 6.6   To execute a power slide, turn around, then extend one skate in your direction of motion. Apply pressure to stop.

DRILLS

Skate and Body Position—Brake Stop

(See Figure 6.1)

Objective: Balance on nonbrake skate while applying brake.

Location: Nonrolling surface (grass or carpet).

1. Focus on an object 15 to 20 feet in front of you.
2. Square your shoulders to the direction you're facing.
3. Put your arms up in front of you, chest high.
4. Move your skates into an extended length stance with the right skate forward.

5. Shift your body weight to your left skate and lower your rear end.
6. Lift the toe of your right skate until you feel pressure on the brake.
7. Maintain balance in this position.
8. Practice moving from a gliding position to the brake position several times.

Brake Stop

(See Figure 6.1)

Objective: Stopping with the brake.

Location: Flat, open, hard, rolling surface.

1. Put on all safety gear as described in chapter 2.
2. Execute three consecutive stroke and glide combinations.
3. Move into the extended length stance with the right skate forward.
4. Shift your body weight to your left skate and lower your rear end.
5. Lift the toe of your right skate, apply pressure on the brake.
6. Stop.
7. Practice several times, gradually increasing speed.

Skate and Body Position—T-Stop

(See Figure 6.3)

Objective: Balance on nonstopping skate.

Location: Nonrolling surface (grass or carpet).

1. Focus on an object 15 to 20 feet in front of you.
2. Square your shoulders to the direction you're facing.
3. Put your arms up in front of you.
4. Bend your left knee and ankle forward.
5. Shift your body weight to your left skate.
6. Move your right skate behind your left skate at a 90-degree angle.
7. Apply downward pressure to the wheels on your right skate.

T-Stop

(See Figure 6.3)

Objective: Stopping.

Location: Flat, open, hard, rolling surface.

1. Put on all safety gear as described in chapter 2.

2. Execute three consecutive stroke and glide combinations.
3. Bend left knee and ankle forward.
4. Shift your body weight to your left skate.
5. Move your right skate behind your left skate at a 90-degree angle.
6. Apply downward pressure to the wheels on your right skate.
7. Stop.
8. Practice several times, gradually increasing speed.

Y-Stop

(See Figure 6.4)

Objective: Stopping.

Location: Flat, open, hard, rolling surface.

1. Put on all safety gear as described in chapter 2.
2. Execute three consecutive stroke and glide combinations.
3. Bend your left knee and ankle forward.
4. Shift your body weight to your left skate.
5. Move your right skate behind your left skate at a 45-degree angle.
6. Apply downward pressure to the wheels on your right skate.
7. Allow the left skate to turn to the right, so your body pivots around the right skate.
8. Slowly spin to a stop.

Hockey Stop

(See Figure 6.5)

Objective: Stopping.

Location: Flat, open, hard, rolling surface.

1. Put on all safety gear as described in chapter 2.
2. Execute three consecutive stroke and glide combinations.
3. Move your right skate slightly forward into an extended length stance.
4. Execute a sharp right turn; push hard against the skates so they slide across the skating surface.
5. Stop.

Power Slide

(See Figure 6.6)

Objective: Stopping.

Location: Flat, open, hard, rolling surface.

1. Put on all safety gear as described in chapter 2.

2. Execute three consecutive stroke and glide combinations.
3. Begin to execute a Y-stop and turn backward.
4. While turning backward shift your weight to your left skate and slide your right skate out in your direction of motion.
5. Stop.

Common Mistakes and Correcting Them

1. Pivoting or turning around brake when stopping: Your stance is too wide (see Figure 6.7). The braking skate must be directly in front of you when stopping or you'll pivot around the brake. Review "Width" on page 48.
2. Pivoting or spinning when setting down drag skate: Drag skate is not at a 90-degree angle to your direction of motion. Set your skate down directly behind the forward-facing skate at a 90-degree angle. (Pivoting to a stop is called a Y-stop; see "Advanced Stops.")

Figure 6.7 If your stance is too wide when you execute a brake stop you will rotate around the brake.

REMEMBER

1. Brake stop.
2. T-stop.
3. Y-stop.
4. Hockey stop.
5. Power slide.

 *CHAPTER 7*

Turns

Executing consistently smooth turns on in-line skates is one of the most rewarding parts of skating. Most skiers will tell you that carving long fluid turns through a field of fresh powder is the best part of skiing. Many in-line skaters experience the same feeling while carving turns on their skates.

The Leading Skate

The extended length stance is the key to successful turns. When coasting with one skate in front of the other, the skate in front will lead you into the turn. If you want to turn right, your right skate should be forward; to turn left, your left skate should be forward. Another way of describing this is "inside skate forward." The skate on the inside of the turn is forward (see Figure 7.1).

Figure 7.1 When turning, maintain an extended-length stance, with the skate closest to the turn direction forward.

If you're not comfortable coasting in the extended length stance with either skate forward, go back to chapter 4, page 52 and practice alternating the forward skate.

You may have already developed a habit of turning with the outside skate forward. This is common among skiers who have learned to turn with the outside ski forward. If you do turn in this manner you'll need to spend time relearning and breaking the habit. This is not always easy, but it's worth the effort to ensure more stability and control while skating.

The Mechanics of Turns

Before you begin practicing turns, it is important to understand some of the techniques that are involved in executing them.

Edges

Skiers and ice skaters are familiar with the concept of using edges in turns. The wheels on in-line skates have no edges, but they do have the rounded sides of the wheels, which grip the skating surface very well (see Figure 7.2).

Learn to trust your skates. The wheel design on in-line skates allows you to lean the skate over without it slipping out from under you.

Figure 7.2   In-line wheels will stick to the ground even when you're leaning into a turn.

Leaning Into the Turn

To turn successfully on in-line skates you must lean into the turn. It is nearly impossible to make an efficient turn without leaning into it. This forces your skates to be at an angle, so your body will not be vertical over your skates; it will lean in slightly, in the direction of the turn (see Figure 7.3).

Figure 7.3   You must lean in to carve smooth turns.

Where to Look

Your eyes should always be looking in the direction you want to go. If you're looking down at your skates, you cannot be preparing for the next turn. Look in the direction of your turn. If you're turning left, look left. Your body goes where your eyes go.

Shoulders Turned In

Turn your shoulders in the direction of the turn and drop the inside shoulder slightly. If you're turning to the right, turn your shoulders to the right, and drop your right shoulder slightly. This will force you to lean into the turn.

Favored Direction

It's common for skaters and skiers to favor turning in one direction more than the other. Practice until you are confident turning in either direction.

Connecting Turns

After you have gained confidence in turning both to the left and right you will want to begin connecting turns. This is the beginning of truly fun in-line skating. These fundamental skills will be used in all types of advanced skating.

Transition of Forward Skate

The key to connecting turns is changing the forward skate after the preceding turn is completed. If you begin with a left turn, the left skate is forward and you are leaning to the left. As you come out of the turn, straighten your body to a vertical position and shift your stance until your right skate is forward and leads you into the right turn (see Figure 7.4a-d).

For information on changing the forward skate, refer to the chapter 5 drill "Coasting: Extended Length Stance." Practice alternating your forward skate while coasting.

Maintaining Proper Posture

Proper posture remains important as your turning skills develop. As you make the transition from one turn to the next, maintain the for-

Figure 7.4a,b,c,d Start turning left with the left skate forward (a); lean to the left (b). Straighten to a vertical position and shift your right skate to the forward position (c); lean into a right turn (d).

ward bend in your knees and ankles. Remember that your inside, or forward, knee will have more forward bend and will lead you into and through the turn.

Increasing Speed

As you gain confidence in turning you will approach turns with more speed. With increased speed you will have to change three things to maintain the same arc through a turn.

1. Extend the length of your stance. Move your forward skate farther forward and your back skate back a little more. This will require more bend in the forward knee and the back ankle.

2. Lower your body closer to the ground. This will allow you to

complete faster turns. The lower your center of gravity is, the faster you can turn.

3. Increase weight and pressure on the inside leg. As you enter a turn, your forward knee will push down, into the turn. You will feel more pressure applied to the knee on your forward leg. This becomes a more aggressive posture as you are forced to drive the forward knee into the turn.

As you practice these turns, remember: Chances are good that you have not reached the limits of your skates and they will not slide out from under you. There is a limit to how far you can push the skates, but most skaters do not reach that limit until they dramatically increase their speed.

Crossover Turns

The crossover turn is a combination stroke and turn that is utilized in roller skating, ice skating, and in-line skating (see Figure 7.5). The benefit of the crossover is increased speed while turning. Crossovers can be broken down into three different segments: the stepover, the understroke, and the top stroke. Remember that the crossover is executed during a turn and not while coasting in a straight line.

Figure 7.5 In a left crossover turn the left skate pushes out underneath the body to the right; the right skate steps over to the left.

Balance

The crossover requires balancing on one skate while turning and then alternating which skate you're balanced on. This may sound intimidating, but you can learn the crossover one step at a time.

In chapter 5, "Stroke and Glide," you learned that you can balance on one skate while the other skate is extended in the stroke position.

A crossover is different in that the skate you are balanced on is carving the arc of a turn and stroking at the same time. Crossovers require constant body movement, shifting bodyweight, and balance.

Stepover

In turning, the inside skate is under the hip and slightly forward of the body and the outside skate is behind. In the crossover, your weight is shifted to the forward skate; the back skate is picked up and crossed over, in front of and slightly inside the previously forward skate. ''Inside'' means closer to the center of the turning arc. In other words, the stepover skate is not set down directly in front of the under stroke skate but slightly inside of it (see Figure 7.6).

Figure 7.6 A forward bend in the knee and ankle will make the stepover easier.

The term *crossover* comes from this first step of the outside skate, as it crosses over and in front of the other skate. In a left turn, your left skate should be forward and leading through the arc of the turn. Shift your weight to your left skate. Pick up right skate and step over and in front of your left skate; set it down forward and slightly inside of your left skate.

Understroke

The understroke is not a required maneuver to complete a crossover, but it is an important part of the crossover and has many benefits. You can complete the crossover step simply by stepping over as already described and not stroking underneath your body.

The understroke is one of skating's most powerful and efficient strokes. It takes time and practice to learn a powerful understroke, but most advanced skaters agree that it's one of the most used methods of increasing speed.

The understroke is a portion of the crossover turn that is executed at the same time as the stepover. It pushes underneath your body in the opposite direction that your stroking leg would normally push.

Under normal stroke and glide conditions your left leg strokes out to the left of your body. In a left crossover turn your left leg will stroke underneath you, towards the right side of your body (see Figure 7.7).

Figure 7.7   The understroke is the most powerful part of the crossover turn.

The understroke occurs simultaneously with the stepover; as you complete the understroke, shift your weight to the skate that has just completed the stepover.

Top Stroke

Upon completion of the stepover and understroke shift your weight to your stepover skate. The understroke skate moves back to the original side of the body and the stepover skate begins to push out in a normal stroking direction. This is called the top stroke.

Let's continue with the example of a left crossover turn; your weight has been shifted to your right skate upon completion of the stepover. Your left, understroke skate begins to recover to the left side of your body and your right skate begins to push out, to your right, to complete the top stroke (see Figure 7.8).

As you execute the top stroke with your right skate, shift your weight to your left skate. Pick up your right skate and go directly back into the crossover step.

These crossover steps can be quick short steps or fully extended long strokes depending on your turning radius, speed, and desired acceleration. Figure 7.9a-d shows each section of the crossover turn.

Crossovers can be executed at any time during a turn. Remember

Figure 7.8 The top stroke is completed by the same skate that does the stepover. Push out and away from your body.

Figure 7.9a,b,c,d The crossover turn is a complex maneuver. Get into position (a). The top stroke (b), stepover (c), and understroke (d) overlap each other.

the fundamentals you have learned. Keep your weight forward on the balls of your feet, look in the direction of the turn, and angle your shoulders into the turn; your inside skate still leads. Stay relaxed and practice.

Traversing Down Hills

Traversing on hills is a technique adapted from skiing that allows in-line skaters to maintain control of their speed while skating down hills. Traversing is a series of connecting right and left turns that allow you to skate across a hill instead of straight down it.

To help understand traversing, imagine yourself standing at the top of a wide cement hill. If you were to drop a ball and let it roll to the bottom of the hill, gravity would pull it down the hill. Imagine that the ball left a line where it rolled; this is called the fall line. It's the fastest route down the hill.

If you were to coast down the hill on your skates, you would follow the same line. Traversing will allow you to slow your descent. The key is to crisscross back and forth across the fall line (see Figure 7.10). This is called traversing. You are traversing across the fall line, rather than skating with it.

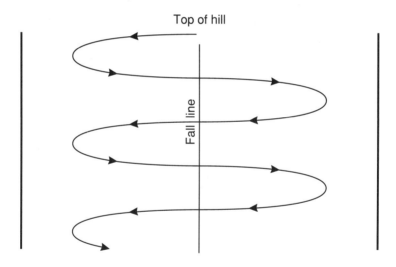

Figure 7.10 The straight line down the hill is the fall line, the fastest route to the bottom. The crisscross or traversing line is the way to control speed down hills.

Skate across the side of a hill, then make a 180-degree turn and go back in the opposite direction. After crossing the hill execute another 180-degree turn and head back in the original direction. Continue the zigzag pattern to the bottom of the hill.

If you begin to gain too much speed while traversing you can turn more than 180 degrees and actually skate up hill slightly. This will reduce your speed.

DRILLS

Basic Turns

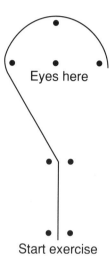

Eyes here

Start exercise

Figure 7.11 Place markers on the ground to practice turns from both directions. Maintain a consistent turning arc around the markers.

Objective: Execute right and left turn.

Location: Flat, open, hard, rolling surface with markers, as shown in Figure 7.11.

1. Execute three consecutive stroke and glide combinations.
2. Move into the extended length stance with your right skate forward.
3. Begin to lean into the turn.
4. Lower your right shoulder slightly.
5. Keep your eyes on the center marker.
6. Maintain a smooth carving turn around the arc of the cones.
7. Practice a left turn; your left skate leads into the turn.

Connecting Turns

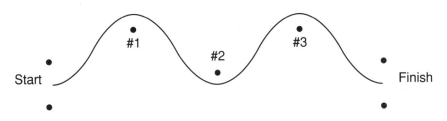

Figure 7.12   Place markers to assist in executing connecting turns.

Objective: Connecting right and left turns.

Location: Flat, open, hard, rolling surface with markers, as shown in Figure 7.12.

1. Execute stroke and glide combinations to build speed.
2. Move into the extended length stance with your right skate forward.
3. Execute turn #1.
4. Shift your left skate to the forward position and your right skate back.
5. Execute turn #2.
6. Shift your right skate to the forward position and your left skate back.
7. Execute turn #3.
8. Stop.

Variation: After completing the connecting turns drill you can improve your skill by increasing your speed through the same course. Remember to lengthen your stance and compress your body lower to the ground. Drive into the turn with the inside, forward knee.

Crossover Turns

(See Figure 7.9a-d)

Objective: Execute left and right crossover turns.

Location: Flat, open, hard, rolling surface.

1. Execute three consecutive stroke and glide combinations.
2. Move into the extended length stance with your left skate forward.
3. Begin a coasting turn to the left.
4. Shift your weight to the left skate.
5. Lift the right skate, cross it over and in front of the left skate, set it down.
6. Shift your weight to the right skate.
7. Push under your body and toward the right with your left skate.
8. Begin to return your left skate to normal position.
9. Begin right skate stroke to the right.
10. Set your left skate down and shift your weight to it.
11. Complete the extension of your right skate and lift it. Move right skate directly into stepover.
12. Complete the entire crossover maneuver a second time.
13. Complete the turn and then stop.

Hint: Practice the crossover turn in both directions. In a right turn the stepover is done with the left skate. The understroke is done with the right skate and the top stroke with the left skate.

Common Mistakes and Correcting Them

Figure 7.13 If you turn without an extended length stance, you will not carve smooth, controlled turns.

1. Not able to maintain arc of turn around markers (see Figure 7.13): Keep your inside skate forward. Lean into your turn.

REMEMBER

1. Right turn, maintain consistent arc of turn.
2. Left turn, maintain consistent arc of turn.
3. Right and left turn with increased speed.
4. Connecting right and left turns.
5. Crossover right turn.
6. Crossover left turn.
7. Traversing down hill.

◯◯◯ CHAPTER 8

Putting It All Together

In-line skating is a sport of changing conditions. Speed, terrain, body position, and posture all can change at any time. You have learned the skills that will allow you to adapt to these changes.

Now you must learn to put all of the fundamentals together in a manner that allows you to quickly and confidently adjust to changing conditions. There is one key to developing this skill—practice!

Practice

Nothing will accelerate your learning curve faster than time on your skates. Find time to skate, relax, and enjoy your newfound sport. To maximize your practice time, create a practice course that incorporates all the skills you've learned. A drill for practicing appears on page 89.

Changing Conditions

The skills that have been taught in previous chapters are not always strict rules of skating technique. Under some conditions they will require minor changes. The following sections describe some of these.

Up Hills

When skating up hills you should shift your weight back on your skates slightly (see Figure 8.1). This is a change from your normal skating posture of having your weight over the balls of your feet. It will allow you to coast up the hill with less resistence, aiding you in creating the maximum amount of forward motion with the least amount of energy. If you're skating up a steep hill, use a shorter than normal stroke and try to maximize your glide time.

Figure 8.1 When skating up a hill, shift your weight back slightly more than normal.

Down Hills

Skating down hills creates challenges that can be intimidating. Deciding how to stay in control when skating down a hill requires an analysis of the hill and your skating skills. You must consider: Is the hill wide enough to traverse? Will the brake keep my speed down enough so I don't crash into a telephone pole at the bottom? If I begin to go too fast, or lose control, what should I do?

If you are faced with a hill that is above your skill or confidence level, take your skates off and walk to the bottom. Better safe than sorry. Skate smart!

Curbs

It's common to have to go up or down curbs while in-line skating. With a small amount of practice, you should not be intimidated by curbs.

Up Curbs.   Going up a curb on in-line skates is no different than going up a curb while walking or running. As you approach the curb, shift your weight to one skate and lift the other skate and step onto the curb (see Figure 8.2). When the skate is on the curb shift your weight to it and lift the back skate up.

Figure 8.2 Shift your weight to one skate and lift the other up and over the curb.

It's best to practice these step ups slowly at first. As you gain more confidence and you approach curbs at a faster speed, you will need to lift the first skate up sooner and the back skate may actually leave the ground before you set the front skate down.

This transition becomes a small hop in the air. It may sound frightening, but imagine that you are running fast; there are many times when both feet are off the ground. You're making the transition of weight from back to front foot. On in-line skates, this transition is almost identical to running. Practice slowly and build your confidence.

Down Curbs.   When you approach a curb that you must go down, you can either stop and step down the curb, or you can maintain your forward speed and skate off it (see Figure 8.3). If you decide to skate off the curb, approach the curb with both skates on the ground and in the extended length stance for maximum stability.

Figure 8.3   When skating off curbs maintain an extended length stance for stability.

As you go off the curb there is no reason to add any jump; just skate straight off the curb, maintaining the same posture. When you land, allow your knees and ankles to bend forward to absorb the shock of landing. Land with your skates in an extended length stance for additional stability.

Expanding Your Skills

Now that you have a solid foundation of in-line skating skills, you are faced with some decisions. Many skaters will be satisfied with the recreational skating skills that they have developed. They will still have all of the benefits of exercise and a fun new sport. However, many skaters will want to do more.

Where to Learn More

Section III will introduce you to advanced in-line skating and the most well-known special interest areas of the sport: racing, tricks, dance, and hockey. These sections will introduce you and provide instruction on fundamental skills.

The best way to learn the more advanced aspects of in-line skating is to get involved. Check with your local skate shop and find out if they can put you in touch with other skaters who have interests similar to yours. Don't hesitate to contact other skaters and express your interest in learning more. The sport of in-line skating is so new that most skaters are enthusiastic about finding other skaters with similar interests.

Don't just look for other in-line skaters. Some in-line skaters have gotten involved in ice figure skating and funky indoor dance roller-skating and then adapted their new skills to in-lines.

If you don't find what you need, take the initiative and form a practice group or club in your area. In one major U.S. city, skaters formed an informal group to train and practice racing one night a week after work. They attracted as many as 40 people each week, without any publicity.

As your skills increase and your horizons expand, remember that you have developed a solid foundation of skills. Whatever direction you decide to go with your skating, those fundamentals will not change.

DRILLS

Practice Course

Objective: Putting fundamental skills together.

Location: Flat, open, hard, rolling surface with markers as shown in Figure 8.4.

1. Start, stroke and glide.
2. Coasting right turn.
3. Stroke and glide.
4. Coasting left turn.
5. Left crossover turn.
6. Right crossover turn.
7. Stop.

Variation: To add excitement to your practice, try timing yourself or your friends with a stopwatch. Work on decreasing your reaction

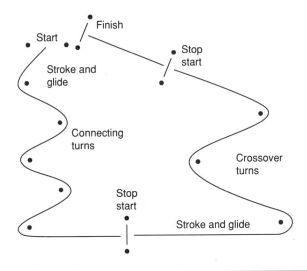

Figure 8.4 This is an excellent course for practicing all skills together.

time to changes in the course. As you practice, you will think less about the maneuvers. They will start becoming automatic.

Up Curbs

(See Figure 8.2)

Objective: Going up a curb while skating.

Location: Flat, open, hard, rolling surface with curb leading to a sidewalk.

1. Start, stroke, and glide.
2. Approach the curb with both skates on the ground.
3. Shift your weight to one skate.
4. Step the unweighted skate above curb level and set it down.
5. Shift your weight to the up skate.
6. Lift the back skate up to follow.

Down Curbs

(See Figure 8.3)

Objective: Going down a curb while skating.

Location: Flat, open, hard, rolling sidewalk with curb leading to a lower surface.

1. Start, stroke, and glide.

2. Approach the curb with both skates on the ground in an extended length stance.
3. Skate off the curb, maintaining the extended length stance.
4. Upon landing, allow your knees and ankles to bend forward to absorb the shock.

REMEMBER

1. Connecting all basic skills—stroke, glide, coasting turns, crossover turns, and stops.
2. Skating up hills—weight slightly back, glide up hill on forward momentum of skates.
3. Down hills—analyze the situation. What is the appropriate speed-controlling technique?
4. Up curbs.
5. Down curbs.

 *PART III*

ADVANCED IN-LINE SKATING

Millions of people around the world are enjoying the recreational and health benefits of a new sport. Some, after learning the fundamentals, want to expand on those skills and explore more advanced types of skating.

Advanced in-line skating can be divided into three primary disciplines: racing, tricks and dance, and roller hockey. In this section we'll introduce you to each.

CHAPTER 9

In-Line Racing

Visualize yourself on your skates at the start of a 10K race. Five hundred other skaters are waiting for the gun, and thousands of spectators line the course to cheer you on. The starting gun sounds, and it's a wild sprint for the first hundred yards as skaters jockey into position. Several pace lines form—groups of skaters gliding stride for stride only inches apart. The leaders create a draft for everyone to follow. You can't believe how easy the draft makes it to stay in the pack.

After several miles your pack of skaters thins out as some tire and drop off the pace. You find yourself maintaining the pace and wondering who is more tired, you or the skaters around you. Suddenly a couple of skaters overtake you from behind. You reach inside for the extra energy to catch up, but you look behind to see that you're leading ("pulling") a pace line (see Figure 9.1). To conserve energy you back off to let someone else move in front to break the wind.

Figure 9.1   Leading a pace line uses 20% more energy than following.

Wheels humming, wind whistling, legs striding in unison. In a cooperative effort to conserve energy the lead switches every 30 seconds or so. Your pack works together to catch the lead pack. With a mile and about 2-1/2 minutes to go, your pack sails past the lead pack. You see other skaters sprint behind you to catch up. You smile, knowing you're conserving energy while others are using theirs up.

You're fifth in a pack of nine skaters. You find yourself looking around, wondering who will have the most energy left for the final sprint. The speed and rhythm of the pack increase as you approach the last half-mile.

You can't stand it any longer. You jump out of line and start your sprint for the finish. The leaders are caught off-guard as you pass them on your way to the front. With 100 yards to the finish you're at top speed and the crowd is roaring! Everyone is sprinting for the line, and you catch a glimpse of a skater on your right. Passed by three skaters right at the finish line, you end up with a solid fourth place and speculate, "Maybe I started my sprint too soon. Guess I've learned a lesson for the next time."

Types of Racing

Most outdoor races have beginner and advanced divisions, so don't let the idea of competition dissuade you from trying an in-line race. Whether your intention is to win or just enjoy a day of organized skating, a goal shared by all skaters is to have fun!

As the sport of in-line skating grows, so does the interest in racing and competitions. Over the last few years people ranging from 5 to 75 years old have tested their endurance and skills against the clock and each other by competing in races from 100 meters to more than 100 miles. Almost every major U.S. city holds at least one in-line skating race a year, and that number is sure to grow. For more information on race schedules, contact IISA and USAC/RS at the addresses listed in the appendix.

If you desire to get involved with in-line racing, read on to learn about the competitive aspects of the sport and how to train for them.

Sprints

Sprint racing requires a high-speed burst of energy from a standing start. Distances are usually 300 to 1,500 meters, with competitors racing against the clock rather than each other.

10-Kilometer Races

The 10K is by far the most popular distance for in-line racing. This is a 6.2-mile race that is usually conducted on a closed circuit course similar to criterium style bike racing (see Figure 9.2). Competitors form "pace lines" to cut down wind resistance and conserve energy. This style of racing is exciting for both participants and spectators; the race combines strength, speed, endurance, and strategy.

Figure 9.2 Most 10Ks are raced on a closed-circuit, criterium-style course.

There have been 10Ks in the United States with more than 1,000 competitors in a single race, and the majority of them finish in less than 45 minutes. The fastest skaters complete the race in less than 17 minutes. That's averaging over 22 miles per hour! Sprints at the end of the race can exceed 30 miles per hour on flat ground.

Marathon and Long-Distance Races

Marathons and long-distance races are growing in popularity as the speeds for 10Ks increase to where they almost become sprints. Longer distance races provide the endurance athlete an opportunity to excel.

Marathons range in distance from the traditional 26.2 miles to more than 100 miles, depending on the particular race. The most well-known marathon in the United States is the annual 85 mile Athens to Atlanta Ultra Marathon, held each October in Georgia. In-line skaters have completed this race in under 4-1/2 hours!

Indoor Racing

Indoor racing is just opening up for in-line skaters. As mentioned in the appendix, the United States Amateur Confederation of Roller Skating (USAC/RS) has recently legalized in-line skates for indoor competition. This provides a tremendous opportunity for in-line racers who live in regions where bad weather restricts outdoor racing and training.

Indoor racing is different than the outdoor races that we've described. The indoor roller-rink track is usually a 100-meter oval with no more than nine skaters racing at a time. Races are 300 to 2000 meters in length with the most popular being 500 meters. National pace indoor speed skaters on traditional quad skates can skate the 5-lap, 500-meter race in under 55 seconds.

The introduction of in-line skates into indoor-rink racing is having a major impact on this established sport. In-line skates appear to be 20% to 30% faster than the traditional quad speed skates, and in-lines are competing in the same races as quads.

Training for Racing

In-line racing is a sport that you can take as seriously or as casually as you desire. As the sport grows there will be more opportunities for top athletes to receive team sponsorship which will allow them to travel to competitions and win prize money.

In-line racing is becoming a highly visible spectator sport that is attracting sponsorship from major companies around the United States. These sponsorships will help bring the level of competition to new heights, and will put increasing performance demands on the sport's top athletes.

Although this level of athletic aspiration will appeal to only a small percentage of skaters, everyone can benefit from an organized training program. Having specific goals in mind is the first step toward a good training program. Your goal may be to achieve a personal best time for a certain race, or to win your age or skill division. Once you set your goals, the next step is to develop a training program that will fit into your lifestyle and help you achieve those goals.

Developing Your Training Program

Take time to consider the following when developing your race training program.

1. What are your specific goals?

Examples:
   a. To skate a 10K in less than 20 minutes.
   b. To become a better pack skater.
   c. To have a strong sprint at the end of the race.
2. Establish dates for your goals; remember that performance takes time and patience.
   a. First race of the year.
   b. Important races throughout the year.
   c. Most important races of the year.
3. Time dedicated toward training.
   a. Hours per month.
   b. Hours per week.
   c. Hours per day.
   d. Time of day: morning or evening.
4. Establish a starting point and determine your current physical condition.
   a. What kind of shape are you in now?
   b. What is your current best 10K time?
   c. What is your top speed while maintaining coordination?
   d. What is your current maximum heart rate per minute?
   e. What is your current endurance level?

Seven Steps to Quality Training

Most people have work, family, and social obligations to fulfill. These interests and responsibilities leave only so much time for training, but it's the quality of your training that counts, not the quantity.

To achieve maximum quality from your workouts, your program should be divided into the following seven types of training:

1. Flexibility

Flexibility helps create a better flow of blood to the muscles. The more flexible you are, the longer and more powerful your strokes will be. Flexibility will also reduce the possibility of muscle injury or strain. For more information on stretching exercises refer to chapter 3.

2. Cardiovascular Endurance

Your cardiovascular system delivers oxygen to your muscles through the bloodstream. The more oxygen your muscles get, the faster and longer you'll be able to skate. Cardiovascular conditioning is one of the most important parts of your training program; its objective is to increase the size of your heart and how much blood it can circulate. The heart is a muscle that increases in capacity when exercised under the proper conditions.

Increased heart volume is achieved by training at approximately 65% of the heart's maximum beating rate. Training at a higher heart rate will increase the heart's speed but not total blood capacity.

The simplest way to calculate your maximum heart rate is to subtract your age from 220 and multiply by 0.65. A 30-year-old in-line skater who wants to build cardiovascular volume should train at 124 beats per minute ($220 - 30 = 190$; $190 \times 0.65 = 124$). To measure your heart rate while training, you can use a wristwatch-type heart monitor, or take your pulse for 6 seconds and multiply by 10.

3. Technique

In-line racing is not just a sport of strength and endurance; it's a highly technical sport as well. A proficient racer must utilize a long stroke and take maximum advantage of the glide between strokes (see Figure 9.3). The glide is actually rest time; if you skate with proper technique, you can maintain the same speed as a less proficient skater while using less energy.

Figure 9.3 An in-line racer must have a long, strong stroke and stay balanced over the glide skate.

The keys to proper skating technique are balance, coordination, and efficiency. Stay centered and balanced over your glide skate, take long, fluid strokes, and glide between strokes. The only way to improve your technique is to practice.

4. Speed

Speed is how fast you can stroke while still maintaining coordination. High-speed stroking will be utilized during starts, breakaways, and sprints to the finish. A few fast, technically correct strokes can rapidly increase your speed.

A fast stroke is executed with the snap and explosion of the appropriate muscles, with very little glide time in between strokes, while maintaining balance and coordination.

To practice a fast stroke, work on interval sprints of 1 minute each with a one minute rest between sprints.

5. Strength

The more power each of your strokes has, the more rest you can get between strokes. An efficient skater is one who can maintain race speed while using the least amount of energy.

You can build strength by skating up hills or by doing cross-training workouts that put heavier loads on your muscles than skating does.

Examples are weight training, hiking in the mountains, bicycling up hills, or cross-country skiing.

6. Race Strategy

Strategy will vary as the race progresses. A race can be broken down into the start, the pace, the breakaway, and the finish sprint.

The Start.   The start of a large in-line race can be an intimidating event for all but the most experienced racers (see Figure 9.4). Approach the start with the following objectives:

Figure 9.4   Work hard to get a clean start and avoid tripping.

Position yourself in the starting field near racers of similar skill level. If you've been training with skaters who have similar speed and endurance capabilities, start near them.

At the sound of the starting gun, get off the line as fast as possible while avoiding other skaters. The danger here is getting your legs or skates tangled with a competitor and tripping. Pace lines will start to form within 100 yards of the start. It's important to get into the draft of a pace line as soon as possible, to reduce your energy consumption.

The Pace.   The most important part of a good strategic race is using the draft of other skaters (see Figure 9.5). It's difficult for the non-racer to realize how much more efficient you can be while skating in the wind draft of other skaters. Research has shown that a racer in a draft can experience a heart rate 20 beats per minute lower while maintaining the same speed.

With this in mind, it's important for you to feel comfortable and confident while skating in a crowd. The key is to practice and train

Figure 9.5 Staying in a draft line will reduce energy consumption.

with other skaters. When racing, find a pace line that is skating at a speed you can handle, and stick with that line until the final sprint to the finish or a group breakaway.

The Breakaway. Later in the race, some of the skaters in your pace line will start to fall back as they tire, while others will want to increase their speed. If you want to pick up the pace, it's best to find other skaters in your pack who will go out with you; pick out the skaters who look strong and ask if they want to go faster. It's very difficult to successfully break away on your own because you won't have anyone to draft on or with. Skaters should understand their responsibility to help ''pull'' the line.

Before making your break, skate back in the line for a few minutes until you, and the other skaters who are going to breakaway with you are well rested. When the break is made, make it fast and strong, to catch the pack off guard. Make a clean break. Put enough distance between you and the previous line that it will be difficult for them to catch up.

The Finish Sprint. Most finish sprints start with a gradual acceleration of the pack and increase to the top speed of the skater leading the pace line (see Figure 9.6). Shortly before the finish, individual skaters will break out of the pace line and go for a full-out sprint.

In a close race it's critical to stay in a draft as long as possible to conserve energy. Make your breakaway sprint at the last possible second, allowing yourself enough time to pass the skaters you're trying to beat.

Figure 9.6 Races can be won or lost at the finish sprint.

7. Rest

Allow a recovery period of 36 to 48 hours after every race or intense workout. Without rest, your body won't recover; you'll get run down and fatigued, which makes you more susceptible to getting sick, injured, and burned out. Listen to your body; a tired or sick skater is not a fast one. Get your rest!

You'll be strong in some of these areas, weaker in others. Focus on your weaknesses. Many of these training methods can be combined into the same workout; some will require special focus and take longer to develop. For example, it takes more time to develop your cardiovascular capacity than to develop your speed, but you can work on both at the same time.

Six-Month Training Program

The 6-month training program is designed for those skaters who have already reached a proficient level of skill and conditioning. You should be able to skate at a recreational pace for at least 1 hour without getting tired before beginning this program. The program is the same length as the summer racing season. The objective is to have your best racing performances at the end of the season.

This training program does not include specific mile distances that you should skate, but is adaptable to the types of races you want to train for. The focus is on maintaining a specific heart rate for a specific amount of time. Maintaining the proper heart rate for a designated amount of time will do more to help build your cardiovascular base than just skating a certain distance. For information on calculating your peak training heart rate, refer back to the cardiovascular section in this chapter.

Months 1 Through 3

Objective: Build a strong cardiovascular base and a smooth, consistent technique.

1. Three to four times a week go on long skates of 1 to 2 hours each. Start every workout with stretching and a slow warmup.
2. Maintain approximately 65% of your maximum heart rate. This will allow you to practice proper technique and get a good workout without getting fatigued.
3. When possible, skate with others of similar skill level to help become accustomed to skating in a pace line. Avoid racing each other at this point, as it undermines your training goals.

Month 4

Objective: Increase speed and strength. Attend first races of the season.

1. Go on three skates a week of 30 to 45 minutes each at 80% of your maximum heart rate. If you have trouble maintaining proper skating technique at this heart rate, reduce the length of the workout but maintain an 80% heart rate. Include a 15-minute warmup and warmdown at 65% of your maximum heart rate.
2. Go on one skate a week that includes lots of uphill work, to increase strength.
3. Skate with others.
4. Participate in up to four 10K races. Keep track of your times so you can measure your improvement.

Months 5 and 6

Objective: Achieve racing goals and build towards a peak.

1. Skate as often as possible with other skaters. Push each other to your limits; practice drafting, passing, breakaways, and sprints at the end of simulated races.
2. Skate 45 minutes to an hour, two to three times a week at your

maximum speed while still maintaining proper technique. Find your personal levels of fatigue and recovery. Be sure to get a full day of rest between workouts.

3. Get five days of active rest prior to your final and most important season races. If you skate, do not exceed 65% of your maximum heart rate or skate for more than 30 minutes.

CHAPTER 10

Tricks and Dance

There are several different types of creative skating on in-lines. In this section we take a brief look at artistic, street dance, and radical skating. We also cover some of the fundamental skills that will help you get started with more advanced in-line skating.

Artistic Skating

The United States Amateur Confederation of Roller Skating (USAC/RS) has agreed to allow in-line skates into their competitions. USAC/RS has a complete program called artistic skating that stresses the aesthetic as much as the athletic aspects of skating.

USAC/RS competitions take place in roller-skating rinks and range in size, from local events to World Championships. The artistic disciplines can be broken down into four major categories—dance, figures,

Figure 10.1   Figure skaters from traditional roller skating may begin changing to in-line skates.

freestyle singles, and freestyle pairs (see Figure 10.1). These events are similar to figure skating on ice skates.

It remains to be seen what kind of impact in-line skates will have on this area of USAC/RS. Most artistic roller skaters have used traditional roller skates all of their skating lives, and most in-line skaters have not had the years of disciplined coaching, training, and perfectionism that gain recognition in an artistic competition. For these reasons in-line skates may not have the immediate impact on the artistic USAC/RS events that they have had on racing. However, if you want to learn this type of skating, it's never too late to start. The roller rinks are a perfect place to get started.

Street Dance

Street dance is a type of in-line skating that doesn't really have specific boundaries. This is a freestyle discipline that is a reflection of the individual skater's creativity, skills, mood, and music. It's a music video on in-line skates! Street dancing combines moves from traditional artistic figure skating with contemporary dance steps, and may have a cartwheel thrown in for dramatic effect.

When watching a dance skater, or practicing your own moves, recognize that each move or trick is learned individually and then worked into the skater's routine. Break down the move you want to learn and identify the specific steps that will complete the trick.

Radical Skating, Jumps, and Ramps

As with street dancing, radical skating, jumps, and ramps take their form from different disciplines. Many of the moves that you'll see on in-line skates are adapted from skateboarding and freestyle skiing.

There are in-line skaters who can jump cars from a launch ramp (see Figure 10.2), skate down a flight of stairs, or catch 10 feet of air out of a half pipe! Like all advanced skating, these are dangerous maneuvers that take a great deal of practice to perfect. Analyze each move and the steps that make it work. Wear your safety gear and don't exceed your skill level. Learn one step at a time.

Figure 10.2   Moves on half pipes and ramps are similar to those performed by skateboarders.

Fundamental Skills

The following sections will introduce you to the fundamental skills of trick and dance skating. Many of these skills are used in all forms of creative skating; some, such as skating backward, are used by advanced recreational skaters. As with all skills, the key is practice!

Skating Backward

Skating backward is one of the first things most skaters want to learn once they have mastered the fundamental skills. Skating backward can be intimidating, but it isn't difficult. The basic rules of keeping your knees and ankles bent forward and your weight over the balls of your feet do not change when you skate backward (see Figure 10.3).

The best way to learn to skate backward is to start with your back to the direction you want to go. Stand with the toes of your skates facing slightly in (pigeon-toed); keep your knees and ankles bent for-

Figure 10.3   When skating backward, keep your knees and ankles bent forward. Hands should be in front of you for balance.

ward. To create movement, push both skates out at the same time until they're about 3 feet apart, and then turn your heels in and bring the skates back together. Repeating this movement will create hourglass figures with your skates and propel you backward (see Figure 10.4). Keep your hands and arms out in front of you to maintain balance.

As you become more proficient skating backward you can learn to stroke, one leg at a time, and do crossover strokes while turning. At first, skating backward doesn't feel natural, and many skaters are uncomfortable with it. Stay loose, keep practicing, and you'll pick it up.

Toe–Heel Glide

The toe–heel glide is another relatively easy maneuver that looks impressive (see Figure 10.5). This trick is done by gliding on the back (heel) wheel of your forward skate and the front (toe) wheel of your back skate. The key to staying balanced is maintaining an extended length stance and keeping your knees bent.

Hourglass skating pattern

Figure 10.4 Your skates will move in an hourglass pattern to create momentum when you start to skate backward.

Figure 10.5 Keep an extended length stance with knees bent when executing a toe–heel glide.

Toe–Toe Glide

The toe–toe glide is slightly more difficult than the toe–heel glide, but it's even more impressive (see Figure 10.6). The toe–toe glide will build strong calf muscles, because a lot of pressure is put on the calves when executing this move. The key to staying balanced is an extended length stance and keeping your knees bent.

Figure 10.6   Maintaining an extended length stance is critical to staying balanced on your toes.

Figure 10.7   Your body follows your nose. Look in the direction you want to spin; turn your shoulders and upper body into the spin.

Spins

Learning to spin on in-line skates takes time and practice, but it's one of the most impressive moves you can perform. Your entire body is part of the spin (see Figure 10.7). To spin, your body must stay centered above your skates while you turn. If your body is misaligned you will not be able to stay on top of the skates.

The easiest way to spin is on the toe wheel of one skate and the heel of the other. It's best to start your spin from a slow-moving or stopped position; forward motion will throw you off your center line. Visually pick a spot on the ground that you want to spin on. As you approach the spot, keep your knees bent. To start the spin, swing your arms and shoulders in the direction you want to spin and look into the spin. Your body will go in the direction your nose goes; in other words, if you're spinning to your left, look over your left shoulder and your body will follow. As long as you keep looking, your body will keep spinning.

Now that your upper body is spinning, the objective is to stay on top of your skates. If you keep your skates flat on the ground the resistance from all of the wheels won't allow you to spin more than a few rotations before you stop. To spin more efficiently, move to a heel–toe stance as you begin to spin. You don't have to lift the heel and toe very far; just enough to keep them from dragging on the ground.

If your wheels left marks on the ground you would see that they're not spinning in one spot, they're spinning in a circle up to two feet in diameter. If you bring your skates closer together your speed of rotation will increase and you will spin longer. This is also true of your arms; as you pull them in closer to your body your speed of rotation will increase (see Figures 10.8a-c).

Spinning takes time and practice. As you become more stable on your skates start your spins with your stance and arms wide, and gradually bring them in to make your body more compact. You'll spin faster and longer.

Artistic Competitions

The trick and dance disciplines of in-line skating have been slow to develop into formalized competitive events. Racing and hockey are well suited to competitive events, but the creative aspects of skating require a much more subjective standard of judging.

This lack of competitive events will undoubtedly change as the International In-line Skating Association becomes more organized and sets standards for artistic competitions. The United States Amateur Confederation of Roller Skating has an established competitive artistic program. As USAC/RS opens its doors to in-line skates, opportunities for in-line skaters will increase.

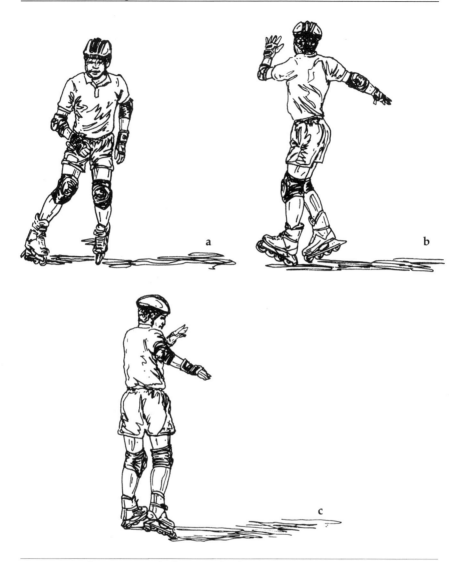

Figure 10.8a,b,c   Approach the spin slowly with a wide stance (a). As you enter the spin, lift the toe of one skate and heel of the other, bring your skates together (b), and twist your upper body into the spin (c).

If you have the skills and motivation to be a trailblazer, both IISA and USAC/RS are avenues you can pursue to help build the future of in-line skates in creative competitions.

DRILLS

Skating Backward

(See Figure 10.3)

Location: Flat, open, hard, rolling surface.

1. Stand with your back to the direction you want to go.
2. Point the toes of your skates slightly in.
3. Push both skates out to about three feet apart.
4. Bring your skates back together.
5. Repeat maneuvers as space allows.
6. As speed increases, coast while skates are parallel.

Common Mistakes and Correcting Them

1. Unable to push skates out: Your knees are not bent; start from a bent knee position.
2. Unable to bring skates back in: Turn heels in slightly.

Toe–Heel Glide

(See Figure 10.5)

Location: Flat, open, hard, rolling surface.

1. Stroke and glide to a comfortable coasting speed.
2. Begin to glide in an extended length stance with at least 18 inches between the front and back skate.
3. Lift the toe of the front skate until you're riding on only the back wheel.
4. Lift the heel of the back skate, keep your knee bent, and ride on the front wheel.
5. Coast in the heel–toe position.

Hint: If you're putting your right skate out in front, you may rub the brake. Try the maneuver with the left skate in front or remove the brake. Before removing the brake, be sure you can properly execute a T-stop.

Toe–Toe Glide

(See Figure 10.6)

Location: Flat, open, hard, rolling surface.

1. Stroke and glide to a comfortable coasting speed.
2. Begin to glide in the extended length stance with at least 12 inches between the front and back skate.
3. Lift the heel of the back skate until you're coasting only on the front (toe) wheel.
4. Lift the heel of the front skate until you're coasting only on the front (toe) wheel.
5. Maintain an extended length stance and keep your knees bent.
6. As your speed slows, drop back to flat skates.

Spinning

(See Figure 10.7)

Location: Flat, open, hard, rolling surface.

1. Visually pick a spot on the ground where you want to execute the spin.
2. Approach the spot with a slightly wider than normal stance.
3. Begin the spin with your eyes, arms, and shoulders.
4. As your upper body begins to twist, lift your skates into a toe–heel position.
5. Maintain balance above your skates.

CHAPTER 11

Roller Hockey

The roots of modern in-line skating are in hockey. In the early 1980s it was ice hockey players, looking for an off-season cross-training work-out, who invented the modern in-line skate. The popularity of in-line hockey is growing at a tremendous rate. Even skaters in cities without a large contingent of ice hockey players are getting involved.

For over thirty years the United States Amateur Confederation of Roller Skating (USAC/RS) has organized indoor roller hockey leagues. This style of roller hockey is traditionally played on quad skates, but, since 1989 in-line skates have been allowed in the USAC/RS hockey programs. USAC/RS sends American roller hockey teams to the World Championships, Pan American Games, and in 1992, for the first time, roller hockey was a sport in the Summer Olympics.

The International In-line Skating Association has stated that one of its objectives is to develop a competitive organization for roller hockey.

The lack of an organized outdoor national league has not kept hundreds of skaters from taking part in regular games around the United States. In this chapter we review the fundamentals of roller hockey and how to organize a team in your community.

Rules

Roller hockey is a competitive team sport that pits two teams against each other for a certain period of time. The objective is to score more goals than the other team. In-line roller hockey has its roots in ice hockey, which is extremely popular in the U.S. and Canada; it's often called the fastest sport in the world, because of the speed at which the puck travels.

The rules of in-line roller hockey have been changed somewhat from ice hockey to make it easier and less dangerous for the players. Official rules have not yet been adopted by the IISA, but the basic rules have been set. The primary rules are as follows:

1. Five players on a team, instead of the six in ice hockey. Two forwards, two defenders and one goalkeeper.
2. No offsides penalty. This allows the players to move freely around the rink and accept breakaway passes from teammates.
3. No body checking. In hopes of attracting a wider group of participants, legal violence has been eliminated.
4. Two periods of 15 minutes each.

Where to Play

Roller hockey can be played in parking lots, roller rinks, basketball courts, tennis courts, and out-of-use outdoor ice rinks. Make sure you're not violating any trespassing rules, and keep the skating suface free of dust, dirt, and oil. Rinks can vary in size, but 180 feet by 85 feet is the most common. A regulation hockey rink is shown in Figure 11.1.

Hockey Gear

Playing hockey on ice or asphalt requires equipment that can stand up to abuse. In this section we identify what components are important and why.

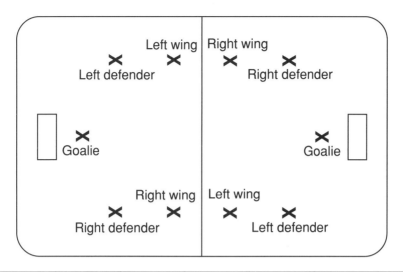

Figure 11.1   Regulation hockey rink and positions.

Skates

Hockey skates need to be constructed of stiff, supportive material (see Figure 11.2). The frames should be short and the wheels set in a rockered position to allow quick turns and skating backwards. Refer to chapter 2 for additional information on hockey skates.

Figure 11.2   Hockey skates should be constructed from durable materials to withstand the abuses of the sport.

Pads

Use all normal protective gear as noted in chapter 2. Goalies should add shin pads, chest pads, face mask, padded gloves, and jock strap for males (see Figure 11.3).

Figure 11.3 Hockey players should wear additional protective gear.

Sticks

Traditional wood hockey sticks can be used, but sticks with a plastic blade have been designed for outdoor hockey (see Figure 11.4). The sticks take more abuse against asphalt or cement than ice.

Puck

There is still some debate about whether the official scoring device will become a ball or puck. If you're playing outside on a rough surface, a low-bounce rubber ball is preferred. If you're playing on a smooth surface you can use a puck with rollers built into it. Both of these are available at most skate shops (see Figure 11.5).

Goals

You can construct your own goals out of PVC pipe and netting. Net size varies from 3-1/2 feet × 5 feet up to ice hockey size, 4 feet × 6

Figure 11.4   Traditional hockey sticks are made of wood; an alternative is one with a plastic blade.

Figure 11.5   A ball or a puck with rollers can be used.

feet. If you don't want to make your own goals, you can purchase them from your local skate dealer.

Basic Skills

Roller hockey requires skills beyond skating. In this section we review the basics of skating, stick and puck handling, passing, and shooting.

Skating

Roller hockey players should have a strong set of fundamental skills, including quick turns, stops, and skating backward. These skills should be developed to the point of being instinctive so you can concentrate on the hockey game. Instruction on these skills appear in the Part II chapters of this book.

Stick and Puck Handling

The hockey stick should be held firmly with both hands (see Figure 11.6). Never lift the blade above your shoulders; this is a violation of the "high stick" rule and is dangerous. You can move the puck by cupping your blade over it and pushing it, or you can push it side to side with the stick. Keep your head up and watch where you're skating; be prepared to avoid opposing defensemen.

Figure 11.6   Hold the hockey stick firmly with both hands.

To increase your puck handling skills, practice skating through an obstacle course while handling the puck. You want to learn where the puck is and how it will react, even without looking down at it. As your skills increase you'll be able to fool your competitors. Act as if you're going to move in one direction and then pass, shoot, or skate in the opposite direction.

Passing

Passing and receiving the puck is an important basic hockey skill. Practice forehand and backhand passes. When passing, anticipate your teammate's forward movement, and pass to where the other player is going to be when the puck arrives.

Shooting

Shooting the puck into the goal is what scores points and wins games. The most popular shots are the wrist shot and the slap shot. The wrist shot is a quick, powerful flick of the wrists that propels the puck off the blade (see Figure 11.7a). In the slap shot, you bring the entire stick back and then quickly forward, slapping the puck (see Figure 11.7b). The wrist shot is usually more accurate than the slap shot but the puck doesn't travel as fast.

a b

Figure 11.7a,b The wrist shot is executed with a quick flip of the wrists (a). The slap shot is faster than the wrist shot, but not as accurate (b).

Shoot at the corners of the goal, toward the open side. Try to make the goalie think you're going to do something other than what you intend.

Positions

Sacrifice and team play are paramount. Hockey requires skill, strategy, and teamwork; you can't all go for the puck at the same time. That's fine for a casual game of street hockey, but it won't win championships.

There are five players on a team: a goal keeper, two defensemen, and two forwards, positioned as shown in Figure 11.1.

Goalkeeper

The goalkeeper has perhaps the most challenging job in hockey: keeping the puck out of the net (see Figure 11.8). The goalkeeper also passes the puck into play.

The goalkeeper must be able to move back and forth quickly in front of the goal and skate forward and backward. The goalie should maintain a slight crouch, elbows out, stick down; skates should be kept parallel to the goal, so the sides of the wheels can be used to block shots. The objective is to block as much of the net as possible.

Figure 11.8 The goalkeeper must keep the puck out of the goal.

Defensemen

The defensemen are responsible for stopping the incoming plays by the opposing team's forwards. They block shots on their goal, clear the puck from in front of the goal, and pass the puck to their forwards. Defenders must be able to skate backward.

Forwards

The forwards are the primary offensive players; they're responsible for moving the puck into the opposing team's territory and setting up plays to score goals. Forwards must have good puck handling skills, including passing, faking, and shooting; they must be in good physical condition, because they skate up and down the rink more than other players. Forwards also take on defensive responsibilities, usually at the beginning of the other team's possession of the puck.

Organizing a Team

Check with the skate shops in your area to see if they can put you in contact with other hockey players. Organize your own team with friends, or post a flier at your local skate shop. As you become familiar with other players in your area, you'll be able to put a team together. For more information on league play, contact the IISA or USAC/RS listed in the appendix.

APPENDIX

Governing Bodies

Most competitive sports are represented by a group called a governing body that takes on many different responsibilities important to that sport. Governing bodies establish competition rules for the sport. They certify judges, referees, instructors, and coaches. They sanction local, regional, national, and international events and competitions. They also protect the interests of the sport from a legal standpoint. Most governing bodies publish newsletters.

These organizations are sponsored by dues-paying members. Most of these members are individual participants, but manufacturers, publishers, and others may also become members.

Many governing bodies contribute financially to the top athletes from their sport. Funds collected from the organization's members are used to help cover athletes' expenses, so they can attend national and international competitions and training camps.

In-line skating is a new and fast-growing sport; its governing body is still in the developmental stage. During the summer of 1991 athletes, manufacturer's representatives, and enthusiasts of in-line skating attended a meeting in Chicago and formed the International In-line Skating Association (IISA), the new governing body of in-line skating.

International In-Line Skating Association

In-line skaters have started to recognize the benefits of the International In-line Skating Association. The objective is to develop a single unified organization to serve the recreational, competitive, and safety needs of in-line skaters worldwide.

A December 1991 press release from IISA states that

the association's objective is to develop programs to promote the safe and courteous use of in-line skates; protect and expand access for in-line skaters to streets, sidewalks, roads, highways, trails and other public places; and to establish a first-rate program of athletic competition for all in-line skating disciplines, including racing and roller hockey. The media has dubbed in-line skating as a potential billion dollar industry and one of the world's fastest growing sports.

A portion of IISA's resources goes toward protecting skaters' rights. IISA has defeated proposed skating bans in several cities around the United States.

The International In-line Skating Association offers membership programs for recreational and competitive skaters, instructors, retailers, event producers, and corporate sponsors. For more information on the IISA contact

International In-line Skating Association
Lake Calhoun Executive Center
3033 Excelsior Blvd.
Minneapolis, MN 55416
(800)FOR-IISA

United States Amateur Confederation of Roller Skating

The United States Amateur Confederation of Roller Skating (USAC/RS, pronounced U-Sack), "is the official National Governing Body for all competitive roller sports in the United States" (in their own words).

USAC was founded in 1937 as part of the Roller Skating Rink Operator's Association and today operates as an independent organization with 23,000 members in the United States. USAC is recognized by the U.S. Olympic Committee, Pan American Sports Organization, and the Federation International de Roller Skating (FIRS), the international governing body for roller skating.

Each year USAC sanctions up to 400 competitions across the U.S. These events are held in three different disciplines: Artistic Skating, Speed Skating, and Roller Hockey. At the end of each season USAC sponsors a national championship in each of these categories.

The focus of USAC has always been traditional roller skates (quads); when in-lines arrived, USAC allowed in-lines to compete domestically, but it was very limited participation. FIRS refused to allow in-line skating in international competition; many indoor roller-rink operators, the foundation of USAC's membership, were reluctant to allow in-line skaters to use their rinks.

During the summer of 1991 FIRS finally agreed to allow in-line skates into their competitions, and USAC immediately responded by sponsoring the National In-line Roller Skating Championship.

For more information on USAC/RS contact

United States Amateur Confederation of Roller Skating
4730 South St., P.O. Box 6579
Lincoln, NE 68506
(402)483-7551

Index